Adonis

عِشْقٌ أَنَا

وَأَتَكَلَّمُ

قَصِيدَةً وَ أُمْضِي

زَهْرُ

شَمْعَةٌ لِلأَرْضِ .

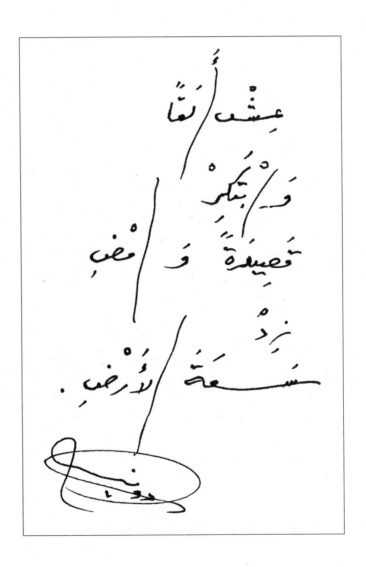

Adonis
Selected Poems

TRANSLATED FROM THE ARABIC BY

KHALED MATTAWA

Yale UNIVERSITY PRESS ■ NEW HAVEN & LONDON

A MARGELLOS
WORLD REPUBLIC OF LETTERS BOOK

Frontispiece: Poem and calligraphy by Adonis.
Translated by Bassam Frangieh.

> Live and be radiant
> Create a poem
> and go away.
> Increase
> The expanse of the earth.

The Margellos World Republic of Letters
is dedicated to making literary works from
around the globe available in English
through translation. It brings to the English-
speaking world the work of leading poets,
novelists, essayists, philosophers, and play-
wrights from Europe, Latin America, Africa,
Asia, and the Middle East to stimulate inter-
national discourse and creative exchange.

Yale University Press books may be purchased in
quantity for educational, business, or promotional
use. For information, please e-mail sales.press@
yale.edu (U.S. office) or sales@yaleup.co.uk (U.K.
office).

Set in Electra type by Keystone Typesetting, Inc.
Printed in the United States of America.

The Library of Congress has cataloged the hardcover
edition as follows:
Adonis, 1930–
[Poems. English. Selections]
Adonis : selected poems / translated from the Arabic by
Khaled Mattawa.
   p. cm. — (A Margellos world republic of letters book)
"Frontispiece: Poem and calligraphy by Adonis.
Translated by Bassam Frangieh"—T.p. verso.
Includes bibliographical references.
ISBN 978-0-300-15306-4 (cloth : alk. paper)
I. Mattawa, Khaled. II. Title.
PJ7862.A519A26   2010
892.7′16—dc22

ISBN 978-0-300-18125-8 (pbk.)

A catalogue record for this book is available from the
British Library.

10   9   8   7   6   5   4   3   2   1

CONTENTS

Printer of the Planets' Books (2008)

A culturally literate person in the Arab world today would find it difficult to recall when he or she first heard of Adonis. By the time one is old enough to drop the names of poets in casual conversation, Adonis is already there among the classical poets 'Antara, Imruulqais, Abu Nawwas, and al-Mutannabi, and certainly among the modern pioneers Ahmad Shawqi, Badr Shakir al-Sayyab, Nizar Qabbai, and Mahmoud Darwish. Later, while browsing the shelves of contemporary literature, one would find copies of Adonis's single volumes of poetry and multi-volume collections occupying sizable space in the poetry section. Eventually, when studying twentieth-century Arab literature, one would discover that Adonis is one of the most original voices in Arabic verse and an indispensable contributor to Arabic criticism. The young lover of literature will pause at the name. What sort of name is Adonis? It is the Greek name of Tammuz, a deity worshipped in the Levant and Mesopotamia prior to the Jews' arrival in Canaan and whose memory was celebrated well into the golden age of Islam. Here the enigma behind the poet's name and his poetry begins to develop—Adonis turns out to be more deeply rooted in the history of the region than its current inhabitants realize.

Born to a modest Alawite farming family in January 1930, Adonis (Ali Ahmad Said Esber) hails from the village of Qassabin near the city of Latakia in western Syria. He was unable to afford formal schooling for most of his childhood, and his early education consisted of learning the Quran in the local *kuttab* (mosque-affiliated school) and memorizing classical Arabic poetry, to which his father had introduced him. In 1944, despite the animosity of the village chief and his father's reluctance, the young poet managed to recite one of his poems before Shukri al-Quwatli, the president of the newly established Republic of Syria, who was on a visit to Qassabin. After admiring the boy's verses, al-Quwatli asked him if there were anything he needed help with. "I want to go to school," responded the young poet, and his wish was soon fulfilled in the form of a scholarship to the French lycée at Tartus, from which he graduated in 1950. He was a good student, and he managed to secure a government scholarship to Damascus University, from which he graduated with a degree in philosophy in 1954. (He would earn a doctoral degree in Arabic literature in 1973 from St. Joseph University in Beirut.)

While serving in the military in 1955–56, Adonis was imprisoned for his membership in the Syrian National Socialist Party. Led by the learned and sophisticated Antun Saadah, the SNSP had opposed European colonization of Greater Syria and its partition into smaller nations. The party advocated a secular, national (not strictly Arab) approach toward transforming Greater Syria into a progressive society governed by consensus and providing equal rights to all, regardless of ethnicity or sect. These ideals, along with the willingness of SNSP's members to confront authority, had impressed the poet while he was still in high school. After being released from prison in 1956, Adonis and his bride, the critic Khalida Said, settled in Beirut and quickly became Lebanese nationals.

There Adonis joined ranks with Yusuf al-Khal in editing *Shi'r* (Poetry) magazine, an innovative Arabic literary journal that was published for ten years and was arguably the most influential Arab literary journal ever. Al-Khal had invited the poet to join him at *Shi'r* after reading one of Adonis's poems while living in New York. In 1960, as Adonis prepared to move to Paris to study on a one-year scholarship, he resigned from the SNSP, convinced that he was not party material. He has not joined a political party since. In Paris he began to translate French poetry and drama, especially the works of Saint-John Perse and Georges Schehade. When he returned to Beirut he resumed his pioneering work with *Shi'r*. From 1970 to 1985 he taught Arabic literature at the Lebanese University; he also has taught at the University of Damascus, the Sorbonne (Paris III), and, in the United States, at Georgetown and Princeton universities. In 1985 he moved with his wife and two daughters to Paris, which has remained their primary residence.

Adonis's publications include twenty volumes of poetry and thirteen of criticism. His dozen books of translation to Arabic include the poetry of Perse and Yves Bonnefoy, and the first complete Arabic translation of Ovid's *Metamorphoses* (2002). His multi-volume anthology of Arabic poetry (*Diwan al-shi'r al-'arabi*), covering almost two millennia of verse, has been in print since its publication in 1964. He has edited several volumes of the works of the most influential writers of Arab modernity, from Yusuf al-Khal to Muhammad Abdulwahab. Adonis's awards include the International Poetry Forum Award (Pittsburgh, 1971), National Poetry Prize (Lebanon, 1974), Grand Prix des Biennales Internationales de la Poésie (Belgium, 1986), Prix de Poésie Jean Malrieu Étranger (France,

1991), Prix de la Méditerranée (France, 1994), Nazim Hikmet Prize (Turkey, 1994), Lerici-Pea Prize (Italy, 2000), Oweiss Cultural Prize (UAE, 2004), and the Bjørnson Prize (Norway, 2007). In 1997 the French government named him Commandeur de l'Ordre des Arts et des Lettres.

Adonis's literary education, guided by his father, was steeped in ancient Arab litera-ture, especially the poetry of the Sufis, whose verses inflamed his imagination with its mystery and explorations of the inner life. Adonis's most noted early efforts had come while he was also under the influence of poets such as Gibran Kahlil Gibran, Ilyas Abu Shabaka, Sa'id 'Aql, and Salah Labaki, all poets who broke from traditional Arabic poetry in tone, subject matter, and prosody. Responding to post-independence disillusionment, the loss of Palestine, or the Nakba of 1948, and the slow rate of social and political progress, Adonis's early poetry attempted to voice his political and social beliefs and to contribute to efforts aimed at pushing Arab culture into modernity. Even at that early age Adonis was merging the classical tradition with the new poetic modes.

By the time he was released from prison and exiled to Lebanon in 1956, the name Adonis—which the poet had adopted during his late teens in response to newspaper editors who rejected his work—had become familiar to readers in Damascus. Later in Beirut, while at *Shi'r*, Adonis wrote many of the magazine's well-articulated and ener-getic editorials, and he played an important role in the evolution of free verse in Arabic.

Adonis and al-Khal asserted that modern verse needed to go beyond the experimenta-tion of *al-shi'r al-hadith* (modern, or free, verse), which had appeared nearly two decades earlier. The *Shi'r* school advocated a poetry that did away with traditional expressions of sentiment and abandoned metrical or formal restrictions. It advocated a renewal of language through a greater acceptance of contemporary spoken Arabic, seeing it as a way to free Arabic poetry from its attachment to classical diction and the archaic subject matter that such language seemed to dictate.

Also responding to a growing mandate that poetry and literature be committed to the immediate political needs of the Arab nation and the masses, Adonis and *Shi'r* energet-ically opposed the recruitment of poets and writers into propagandistic efforts. In reject-ing *Adab al-iltizam* (politically committed literature), Adonis was opposing the suppres-sion of the individual's imagination and voice for the needs of the group. Poetry, he argued, must remain a realm in which language and ideas are examined, reshaped, and refined, in which the poet refuses to descend to the level of daily expediencies. Emerging as one of the most eloquent practitioners and defenders of this approach, Adonis wrote that the poet is a "metaphysical being who penetrates to the depths" and, in so doing, "keeps solidarity with others." Poetry's function is to convey eternal human anxieties. It is the exploration of an individual's metaphysical sensitivity, not a collective political or socially oriented vision.

After leaving *Shi'r* in 1967, and as he prepared to launch *Mawaqif*, a new literary journal, Adonis continued to develop his critique of Arabic poetry and culture. In his 1973 two-volume analysis of Arabic literature, *Al-Thabit wa al-mutahawil* (The fixed and the changing), Adonis theorizes that two main streams have operated within Arabic poetry, a conservative one and an innovative one. The history of Arabic poetry, he argues, has been that of the conservative vision of literature and society (*al-thabit*), quelling poetic experimentation and philosophical and religious ideas (*al-mutahawil*). Al-thabit, or static current, manifests itself in the triumph of *naql* (conveyance) over *'aql* (original, independent thought); in the attempt to make literature a servant of religion; and in the reverence accorded to the past whereby language and poetics were essentially Quranic in their source and therefore not subject to change.

The dynamic, *mutahawil*, current has historically supported rational interpretation of religious texts, emphasizing the connotative over the literal (here Adonis cites the Mu'tazala, Batini, and Sufi religious movements as the persecuted champions of this approach). The literature of the mutahawil current had repeatedly emphasized poetry's esthetic and conceptual impact rather than its moralizing functions, where reliance on fidelity to life and experience as perceived by the individual, rather than on conformity to social standards, is the source of poetic creation.

The shift from naql to 'aql meant that poetry now would be aimed at "embarking upon the unknown, not upon the known." Furthermore, Adonis wrote, "the poet does not transmit in his poetry clear or ready-made thoughts as was the case with much of classical poetry. Instead, he sets his words as traps or nets to catch an unknown world." This kind of open-endedness affects both the poet and the reader. In constructing a world of new words and images the poet has to structure an artistic unit that satisfies his sensibility. In essence, the poet begins using the new language and its imagery until he creates a world he can inhabit.

As for the reader, the ambiguities and indeterminacies in this kind of art (inevitable because of its newness) lead him or her to actively engage in creating mental perceptions of similar innovativeness. The lack of clarity forces the reader to rely not on the writer or the text but solely on his or her mind. For Adonis, who here is as much drawing on the complex esthetics of Abu Tammam as he is referencing Mallarmé, it is this kind of interaction with art, supplemented with unlimited creativity in composition and perception, that Arab culture needs to truly evolve. He argues that a revolution in the arts and in how they are received can generate imaginative strategies at all levels of society. Arabic poetry, he believes, has the responsibility of igniting this mental overhaul in Arab culture. It should not be used to advocate political policies that do not touch the root of Arab cultural stagnation.

Adonis's critique of Arab culture did not merely call for the adoption of Western values, paradigms, and lifestyles per se. Science, which has evolved greatly in Western societies, with its "intuitions and practical results," should be acknowledged as the "most revolutionary development in the history of mankind," argues Adonis. The truths that science offers "are not like those of philosophy or of the arts. They are truths which everyone must of necessity accept, because they are proven in theory and practice." But science is guided by dynamics that make it insufficient as an instrument for human fulfillment and meaning: science's reliance on transcending the past to achieve greater progress is not applicable to all facets of human activity. "What does progress mean in poetry?" asks Adonis. "Nothing." Progress in the scientific sense pursues the apprehension of phenomenon, seeking uniformity, predictability, and repeatability. As such, the idea of progress in science is "quite separate from artistic achievement." Poetry and the other arts seek a kind of progress that affirms difference, elation, movement, and variety in life.

Adonis states that in studying legends and myths, seeking the mystical and the obscure, he found sources that "reveal truths which are more sublime and which concern humanity in a more profound way than scientific truths" precisely because they engage areas that escape the grip of science and rationalism. And thus convinced that rigor and depth—in terms of our knowledge of our psyches and our understanding of our human existence—do not follow the future-oriented outlook of science, Adonis has stressed that progress and modernity in the arts do not follow the chronological order of scientific progress, where greater acquisition of material knowledge often results in human actions or arrangements that contradict humane and progressive thinking. Providing examples of periods of progressive thinking and esthetics in Arab culture, Adonis argues that the "essence of progress is human, that is[,] qualitative not quantitative. . . . Progress is not represented merely by economic and social renewal, but more fundamentally by the liberation of man himself, and the liberation of the suppressed elements beneath and beyond the socioeconomic." Adonis understands progress and modernity as neither linear nor cyclical but episodic, occurring during times when the human mind and imagination are in a dynamic and harmonious relationship with physical needs and concerns.

In this regard, modernity has occurred and can occur anywhere, in the past as well as in the future. Human achievements should not be seen as exclusive to their cultures of origin, for many are among the global attributes of civilization, developments that we have naturally adapted from each other throughout our existence on earth. And while progress emerges from addressing the contradictions and hindrances in a given setting, all human societies can benefit from others' experiences and developments. This is evidenced by our shared instinctive desire to live in physical security and to seek mean-ingful lives. At one point, Arab civilization was best suited to offer this contribution to the rest of humanity, and the West gravitated toward it for all sorts of knowledge and science, just as many Easterners are now gravitating toward the West. Although the products of progressive thinking and renewal can be shared, the onset of renewal in any given society can arise only from a response to the contradictions at hand.

Adonis insists that newness in Arab society and subsequently in Arabic poetry, "how-ever unequivocal its formal break with the past may appear," must be "identifiably Arabic in character. . . . It cannot be understood or evaluated within the context of French or English modernism, or according to their criteria, but must be seen in the context of Arab creativity and judged by the standards of artistic innovation particular to Arabic." The poet therefore needs to be grounded in the organic artistic process that is his native poetry. His expansion of the horizon of human thought and feeling rely in part on the innovations he makes on his medium and his language, where work on their particular facets is the way to expand knowledge in the broadest sense.

Even while viewing Western conceptual innovations with a sense of entitlement, and considering them human cultural advancements, Adonis nonetheless has been a consistent critic of Western societies' and governments' treatment of the rest of humanity. The fiercely anti-totalitarian Adonis has repeatedly asserted that Western weaponry, industry, and capital have dehumanized both Westerners and those subject to their violence and greed. His critique of the damaging effects of mechanization and the "mongrelizing" force of globalization have become increasingly acerbic in the last two decades, coinciding with his relocation to Paris in 1985.

Adonis's visits to Arab capitals, where he is often asked to lecture on the state of Arab culture, have often caused controversies. To young Arab poets who have adopted free verse, which he has long advocated, he says that their work is only superficially modern, as its outlook is often trapped in convention. And, causing controversy among wider cultural spheres, he has regularly declared the end of the Arab culture, and the Arabs themselves. Noting that little cultural innovation, let alone science or technology, is being created in the Arab world, Adonis has harangued Arab audiences in public and in media interviews, accusing them of being mere importers of cultural goods and esthetic styles. Much of Arab music, classical or popular, either reiterates traditional forms or parrots Western styles, he says, and the same goes for most drama, cinema, literature, and visual arts produced in Arab countries. Tinged with a desire to provoke Arab artists and intellectuals to challenge the increasing entrenchment of their societies, Adonis's tone of late never fails to convey a sense of disappointment. He has remained, however, deeply engaged in the affairs of the region and has lent his support to developments that gave him a sense of hope. Feisty, contentious, articulate, and alert throughout his sixty years in public life, Adonis is a well-decorated cultural figure who has refused to rest on his considerable laurels.

Although he is a seasoned and controversial public intellectual declaiming on the state of his society and the world at large, Adonis is first and foremost a poet. And as much as his literary criticism has solidified his role within modern Arabic letters, it is his startling poetry that continues to endow his ambitious esthetic vision. The first two books he published, *First Poems* (Qassa'id ula), 1957, and *Leaves in the Wind* (Awraq fi al-reeh), 1960, presented a well-honed poetic sensibility of great promise, poems in which he resuscitated the tradition of the *qit'a* (poetic fragment). For a long time Arabic poetry has been identified with the classical *qassida*, the odelike lyric-epic in which the poet's biography frames the poem's character and reception. Adonis's early works, represented here with selections from *First Poems*, focus on the poem's voice, directed by related sentiments or events, and in so doing emphasize the poetry at the expense of the poet. It should be noted that Adonis, true to his artistic instincts, never quite adhered to the seemingly programmatic aspects of his vision for Arabic poetry—such as his advocacy of the use of dialect. His language is of a high literary caliber, his diction richer than that of any of his avant-garde peers.

With his third book, *The Songs of Mihyar of Damascus* (Ughniyat Mihyar al-Dimashqi), 1961, Adonis established himself as a unique voice in modern Arabic poetry. Through the persona of the Mihyar, Adonis articulates a vision of the world empowered by revolutionary fervor and mysticism fused with symbolist elements associated with twentieth-century French poetry. The volume also mingles Judeo-Christian-Islamic heritage with Greco-Roman mythology; Mihyar is identified at times explicitly with various figures, including Noah and Adam, and Ulysses and Orpheus. Through this persona, states Adonis, "I wanted to get out of the direct subjective discourse and speak an impersonal language, objective-historical and personal, symbolic, and mythic at the same time. So it is more than a mask; it is a vortex where Arab culture would meet with all its dimensions in the central and pivotal cause: crossing from the old Arab world into the new." In Adonis's words we hear allusions to two cornerstones of Anglo-American modernism: "Vortex" is what Ezra Pound called any dynamic cultural initiative in which an artist moves in a given direction but attempts to survey and affect his or her surroundings. We also hear in Adonis's description of Mihyar an echo of Eliot's "objective correlative," a phrase that encapsulates Eliot's understanding of the French symbolist approach to poetic representation.

Adonis's next volume, *Migrations and Transformations in the Regions of Night and Day* (Kitab al-Tahwulat wa al-Hijra fi Aqalim al-Nahar wa al-lail), 1965, reconstructs the turmoil surrounding the life and legend of Abdulrahman al-Dakhil (731–788 A.D.), the last heir of the Umayyad dynasty, who fled Damascus as the 'Abbasids took control of the caliphate. Al-Dakhil, a figure whose story symbolized youth, betrayal, and people's natural sympathy for the persecuted, traveled westward until he reached Andalusia, where he established an alternate dynastic caliphate and launched one of Islam's most celebrated ages. In both *Mihyar* and *Migrations and Transformations*, Adonis demonstrates mastery of epic scope and lyrical precision. Each of the poems in these two volumes stands on its own while adding a layer to the complex dilemmas facing their speakers. And while Mihyar is a synthetic figure drawn from the region's history and al-Dakhil is based on a specific person, neither of these books renders a narrative as such, both ably demonstrating Adonis's stated preference for circling his subject matter. Mihyar threads through the existential crises of Arab life in the twentieth century and al-Dakhil processes the Arab world's political and cultural crises through the prism of one of its most tumultuous eras. In both books Adonis finds a balance between poetry's sociopolitical role and the demands of the symbolic "language of absence" that poetry required—as he saw it, a language that allowed poetry to focus on perennial points of tension and to endure beyond its occasions.

In *Mihyar* and *Migrations* we find solitude and imagination emerging as powerful forces, uniting within the speaker's mind and lifting him to ecstasy, then separating and forcing him to pit them against each other in order to reunite them. Imagination, coupled with solitude, allows the speaker to witness the transformative capacities of nature, where language is the currency/blood of renewed paradigms. Nature begins to mimic our habits and wear our features, rooting us where we perpetually feel estranged. Without imagination—as in the poem "Adam," as Mihyar recounts the mythical figure's dilemma—solitude is liable to erase all knowledge of oneself. Alternately, the capacity to imagine saves al-Dakhil in his flight from his persecutors, and each encounter with the natural world erases an old longing, creating space for renewal. Similarly, Mihyar, who "is not a prophet/not a star," is nonetheless engaged in dismantling idolized paradigms one by one, replacing them with new discoveries. He embraces the earth by "crawling under rubble," trying to loosen her bond to gods and tyrants. Mihyar is a knight trying to rein in unfamiliar words in "the rough and magical . . . climate of new alphabets." Using irregular rhyme and employing the improvisations on traditional metrics that came to the fore two decades or so before the publication of these books, Adonis here provides musical pleasure without predictability. The subtle musical elements call attention to the language, keeping the reader engaged, but not so enchanted as to be lulled by the music.

In the 1970s, Adonis turned his attention to the long-form poem, producing two of the most original Arabic poetic works of the twentieth century. The first of these volumes, *This Is My Name* (Hadha Huwa Ismi), was first published in 1970 with only two long poems, then reissued two years later with an additional poem, "A Grave for New York." In the poem "This Is My Name," Adonis, spurred by the Arabs' shock and bewilderment after the Six-Day War, renders a claustrophobic yet seemingly infinite apocalypse. Here Adonis is hard at work undermining the social discourse that has turned catastrophe into a firmer bond with dogma and cynical defeatism throughout the Arab world. To mark this ubiquitous malaise, the poet attempts to find a language that matches it, and he fashions a vocal arrangement that swerves and beguiles. Thoughts in "This Is My Name" are so fractured, and loyalty and belief in the collective so fragile, that objects attempt to lure verbs from their subjects to save them from falling into escapist forms of narcissism or black holes of grief. Truthful in its fluidity, the language Adonis employs remains close to nerve endings and refuses to entrust itself to established facts. "I can transform: Landmine of civilization—This is my name," states one of the poem's voices—it's impossible to say that we have a single speaker—declaring that he is a fuse of hope capable of doing away with all that has come before him.

The second long poem, *Singular in a Plural Form* (Mufrad bi Sighat al Jama'), 1975, is a four-hundred-page work. The same breadth of experimentation, linguistic play, and deconstructionist esthetics found in "This Is My Name" permeates the dynamics of erotic union and rupture found in "Body," one of the work's four movements. Wavering between languid serenity and animated joy and disappointment, and between deadpan sobriety and articulate yearning, the lovers in "Body" explore their union's every facet. Doing away with rhyme altogether and opting for syncopated rhythmic patterns and abrupt syntactical transitions, Adonis offers a revolutionary and anarchic flow reminiscent of Sufi poetry and literature. As in the great mystical works that are steeped in eroticism, such as the poetry of Rumi, al-Hallaj, and St. John of the Cross, Adonis's "Body" narrates not a story but the *ahwal* (conditions or states of the heart and soul and the desire to uplift and enhance) of the lovers' struggle for a touch of bliss to dissipate their hefty awareness of mortality.

Adonis's poetry in the 1980s began with a return to the short lyric works exemplified in *The Book of Similarities and Beginnings* (Al-Mutabaqat wa al-Awa'il), 1980. Adonis's work here still carries the scent of a larger project. He is not, as he was in *Stage and Mirrors* (Al-Masrah wa al-Maraya), 1968, holding a convex mirror to current events. Instead, he returns to the beginnings of things, focusing on stages of life and states of mind, imagining a time when one might discern a divide between memory and consciousness, biography and philosophy, and even between innocence and experience. The thrill of these poems is in the crystalline focus that Adonis brings to each subject he addresses, demonstrating that his lyric touch is as powerful as his epic sweep.

The Israeli invasion of Lebanon in 1982 prompted *The Book of Siege* (Kitab al-Hissar), 1985. This work brings Adonis closest to what we might call documentation, and perhaps best demonstrates his oblique approach to narration, in which the lyric of disaster mixes with the prose of somber meditation. The book includes a variety of stunning pieces. "Desert" and "Persons" move in fast-paced montage, slowed by dramatic scenes reminiscent of grainy slow-motion footage with masterful psalm-like passages. The genre-defying "Candlelight" is unique even by Adonis's standards. And "The Child Running Inside Memory" is as pure a lyric as he has ever written. *The Book of Siege*, little known even among Arab readers, is perhaps one of the best war books ever written in Arabic.

Beginning in the late 1980s, Adonis became, at least in his lyric practice, more of a poet of place, as Kamal Abu Deeb notes. Accompanied by his poetic guides, Abu Tammam, al-Mutannabi, Niffari, and Abu al-'Ala al-Ma'ari, the poet travels, seeking zones of openness that parallel the inheritance of progressive and tolerant humanism that he has long championed. Also at this time Adonis began to coauthor books of manifestos with younger poets from other parts of the Arab world (from Morocco to Bahrain) and to collaborate with visual artists and musicians. Exile and the loss of Beirut were thus being replaced by a greater connection to other arts and artists. Adonis's writings in the last two decades demonstrate a deliberate reexploration of the lyric (as exemplified by numerous love poems) and an abandonment of poetry as a unified genre. This era, Adonis once declared, is now simply the age of writing.

In the meantime, Adonis was working on *Al-Kitab* (*The Book*), 1995–2003, a three-volume epic that adds up to almost two thousand pages. In *Al-Kitab*, the poet travels on land and through the history and politics of Arab societies, beginning immediately after the death of the prophet Muhammad and progressing through the ninth century, which he considers the most significant period of Arab history, an epoch to which he repeatedly alludes. *Al-Kitab* provides a large lyric-mural rather than an epic that attempts to render the political, cultural, and religious complexity of almost fifteen centuries of Arab civilization. The form that Adonis opted to use for *Al-Kitab* was inspired by cinema, where the reader/viewer can watch the screen, and where "you see past and present, and you watch a scene and listen to music."

The poet's guide on this land journey is al-Mutannabi (915–965 A.D.), the great poet who was as engaged in the machination of power as he was in being the best poet of his age. The pages of *Al-Kitab* are divided into several parts. One portion of the page relates the personal memory of al-Mutannabi, or what he remembers while walking alongside the poet through history. Another portion is devoted to the guide's individual experience as the poet imagines it. The third, at the bottom of the page, establishes a connection between the two parts, or digresses from them. The book includes a series of homages to the numerous great Arab poets who were killed or exiled and continue to be canonically marginalized. "I was telling my readers that Arab history is more than a history of the sword, that there were also great men," states Adonis. To complete *Al-Kitab* the poet had to read all of the classics of Arab history, making the project an "immense amount of work . . . a crazy undertaking," one that makes it impossible to excerpt in a way that would demonstrate its encyclopedic range and lyrical and dramatic ambition.

After the dense engagement of *Al-Kitab*, Adonis seems to have felt a great sense of relief and a freedom to experiment. Between 2003 and 2008 he published five books, each a deliberate recalibration of the poet's voice. In *Prophesy, O Blind One* (Tanaba' Ayuha al-a'ma), 2003, Adonis, who had been criticized for the lack of personal warmth in his poetry, presents perhaps his most autobiographical chronicles. Hearing Adonis speak in the present tense of our times, telling of his dizzying journeys from airport to airport, American readers may hear supersonic echoes of *Lunch Poems*, which chronicles Frank O'Hara's exuberant midday jaunts through New York City. *Prophesy* also includes an atypical poem for Adonis, "Concerto for 11th/September/2001 B.C." In this idiosyncratic and incisive meditation on the violence unleashed on September 11, 2001, Adonis draws on a sizable segment of recorded human history to review what had become a singular event in our era. Here the poet reiterates and revises his impressions in "A Grave for New York," but not without a sense of anguish that little had changed since the earlier poem, and that little was likely to change in the future. A book published in the same year, *Beginnings of the Body, Ends of the Sea* (Awal al-Jassad, Akher al-Bahr), cross-pollinates two of Adonis's earlier styles, the erotic/mystical atmosphere of "Body" and the lyrical quickness of *The Book of Similarities and Beginnings*. The poems in *Beginnings of the Body* utilize sharp imagery, dialogue, and quiet musings within a formal consistency that unites them into a powerful meditation on love.

Among the more recent books is *Printer of the Planets' Books* (Warraq Yabi'u Kutub al-Nujum), 2008, which, with its leisurely prose meditations interspersed with lyrical flashes, draws on the poet's memories, especially his childhood in Qassabin. Tender and poised, these poems never veer into nostalgia or sentimentality. Adonis adroitly recaptures a child's sense of wonder, as well as his anguish and fears. Above all, perhaps, these poems capture the villagers' dignity, empowered by a naturally philosophical outlook and a practical resourcefulness that complement each other. The volume ends with a poem to poetry, or to the muse, who has visited him for years, always wearing the same black dress. Poetry has served the poet well in its all-consuming fashion, allowing him for decades "to fall asleep fatigued between the thighs of night" and to reinvent himself with every visit. But now he longs for a change; he wishes for poetry that would surprise him. The poem is a masterful end to the book and a brilliant subtle comment on the poet's vision of his future poetry and career.

Adonis's desire for renewal is not surprising. Looking at his oeuvre as presented here, we note the creativity and the great sense of liberty with which he went about inventing himself, in formal and prosodic aspects, and in tone and subject matter. We also note a great capacity for cunning, where creative impulses are embraced but are made to work hard for the poet's acceptance. Like al-Ma'ari before him, the poet maintained his skepticism of all forms of enthusiasm, and waited for his ideas to prove their mettle. Like Abu Tammam, who, when asked, "Why do you not write what is understood?" replied, "Why do you not understand what is written?" Adonis has entrusted language with the role of stretching our conceptual faculties while trusting the reader's natural ability to occupy new realms of thought out of sheer curiosity. Finally, like al-Mutannabi, Adonis seems to have learned to speak with the full force of his art, having forged it with the heat of his doubt and creativity, and even his most ambiguous utterances exude clarity. Adonis is a poet who takes risks, but they are calculated ones taken when the stakes are truly high and requiring every ounce of the poet's creativity and intellect. Fortunately for readers of Arabic poetry, the rewards have never failed to bring them face to face with the sublime.

Works Cited

Adonis, *Al-Thabit wa al-Mutahawil* [The fixed and the changing] (Beirut, 1977).

Adonis, *Introduction to Arab Poetics*, translated by Catherine Cobham (Austin: University of Texas Press, 1990).

Adonis, "There are Many Easts in the East and Many Wests in the West," interview with Margaret Obank and Samuel Shimon, *Banipal* 2 (June 1998): 30–39.

Adonis, *Al-Adab*, vol. 4, no. 4, 1962, quoted in Shmuel Moreh, *Modern Arabic Poetry 1800–1970: The Development of Its Forms and Themes Under the Influence of Western Literature* (1976).

Mounah Abdallah Khouri, *Studies in Contemporary Arabic Poetry and Criticism* (Ann Arbor: University of Michigan Press, 1987).

A NOTE ON THE TRANSLATION

A few weeks ago I found a letter from Adonis in which he thanked me for translating two short poems by him that appeared in *Al-Ahram Weekly,* Egypt's most widely distributed English-language newspaper. He also stated that he had no objection to my request to assemble and translate a selection of his more recent work. The letter was sent on April 13, 1992. At the time I contacted Adonis I had translated most of his *Celebrating Vague-Clear Things* and felt empowered to go on with more work. However, I soon realized that this work, with the particularity of its Arabic references, could not stand on its own in English without much of the poet's other work providing context. I also realized that to assemble a volume of more recent works I needed to work through at least twenty years of poetry. And, further, I had a ways to go before making any claims to being a poet myself. I could not bring myself to write the poet about my disappointing realizations, perhaps aware that he is accustomed to my kind of exuberant enthusiasm.

As I read more of Adonis's work over the years, in the original and in translation, I felt repeatedly that only a large of selection of work could give a sense of the myriad stylistic transformations that he had brought to modern poetry at large, through his esthetic renderings of the cultural dilemmas confronting Arab societies in particular. Thirteen years after receiving his letter, and after completing several translation projects, I picked up Adonis's collected poems and began to translate, this time beginning with the earlier poems. I did not tell the poet that I was working on his poems, as I was still unsure that I'd do him justice. I vowed to contact him only when I had a substantial selection to offer. In 2006, when I was about to begin translating "This Is My Name," I was contacted by editors at Yale University Press who were interested in assembling the volume that I'd dreamed up way back in 1992. Furthermore, the editors said, Adonis had suggested that they contact me for the task. This was a chance that I did not want to miss.

Many questions arose as I began to contemplate the selection of work. Since a sizable representation of Adonis's early work had been translated lucidly and lyrically by Samuel Hazo and Abdullah al-Udhari, I intended to minimize retranslation, if only to increase the total availability of the poet's work in English. Shawkat Toorwa's translation of *A Time Between Ashes and Roses* and Adnan Haydar's and Michael Beard's translation *Mihyar of Damascus: His Songs*—both from Adonis's early to middle period—necessitated that I forgo all anxieties about repeat translation and forge ahead, selecting what I perceived to be the best of the poet's work.

While keeping in mind a balance between his most critically acclaimed poetry with work that would show the continuum of his evolution as a poet, I also focused on what I could translate in a way that satisfied me as a reader of English verse. The matter of choosing was based on the English results, along with the goal of representing the majority of the poet's books. And so, with only a few exceptions, all of Adonis's seminal works are represented here. I hope that the arc of his development as a poet, and the continued broadening of that arc, are amply evident.

Avid readers in Arabic, however, will note that this selection includes no poems from Adonis's second book, *Leaves in the Wind* (Awraq fi al-reeh), 1960. This book falls between the first selection of poems (*First Poems*) and *Mihyar*, the poet's first significant early work, but does not seem to constitute a discernable development in the poet's unique voice. Readers also may question the absence of *Al-Kitab*, Adonis's three-volume, fifteen-hundred-page late work. *Al-Kitab*, as Adonis himself recently noted, "is very difficult to understand for someone without a very good grasp of Arab history." How to excerpt such a work in a decidedly limited space was, at first, a beguiling challenge. Eventually, however, I became convinced that no small sample of *Al-Kitab* would offer an adequate sense of the work's scope, and that the absence of the work is a better indicator of its magnitude than any reductive sampling of it would be.

The other gap is the exclusion of two of Adonis's books published in this decade. Here my choices were more decisive. None of the five books that Adonis had published between 2003 and 2008 can be seen as a separate development in his sixty years of poetry, despite the range of subject matter. Each of these books can be seen as a deliberate recalibration of the poet's voice, but to include them all would have overloaded the book and perhaps presented a lopsided image of the poet's development. I have chosen three books that demonstrate the breadth of Adonis's work and his voracious appetite for experimentation. *Printer of the Planets' Books*, firmly reminding us of the poet's roots and his continued attachment to poetry, has an intimacy that helped round out this selection. In noting the stylistic and thematic variety of these late books combined, the reader will, I hope, see how open-ended and self-regenerative Adonis has been.

The language of modern Arabic poetry, especially when coupled with metrical elements, rings a few notches above middle diction. It can step into poetic or even archaic diction yet not seem to readers archaic or even too obviously allusive or overly self-conscious. Perhaps the last time English could do something akin to what Arabic poetry is doing today was in the hands of T. S. Eliot, Hart Crane, and Wallace Stevens, a language that believed in its alterity and trusted its formal bearing. But what American poet now can mimic Eliot and Crane and not sound derivative? American readers reading Adonis, especially in "This Is My Name," perhaps should try to imagine that his poetry has that formal high-modernist lilt.

As a translator and as a poet who only occasionally steps into formal diction, I felt that my own style and inclinations needed to be the base from which I would begin this project. I felt sure that as I translated more of Adonis's poetry I would grow with the poet and develop a harmonious accommodation of style, listening to the words I'd chosen and comparing them with the literal meaning of the originals and trying to weigh them emotionally to find the appropriate tone and cadence. In this process I was aided by recalling a conversation I had with Adonis in which we briefly talked about his own translation process. I had asked him about the critics who attacked his work. "These critics claimed that I erred in the literal sense," Adonis explained, "but I did not, I believe, make any poetic errors. That I could not allow myself to do." I took this advice as a vision for this translation project, the most difficult one of the nine I have undertaken.

I have been asked often about translation approaches and strategies but have become increasingly mystified about how to answer. In essence, I am not capable of describing the methodology of this translation project or any before it, as I believe it is impossible to determine a method of translating a work, particularly one of poetry. As my old teacher Willis Barnstone astutely notes, deciding on one approach to translating a work will only prove frustrating. Sooner rather than later, the translator will end up breaking any promises he has made about his method or process. And determining what one's approach had been after the project is complete is like trying to describe a long journey with a single episode in it. In this regard I take it for granted that these translations of Adonis's poetry are neither literal nor so flexible as to stray from the literal content of the poem. The methods I have used to match fidelity with artistry are basically all the means I could muster.

Much of Adonis's early poetry makes frequent use of rhyme, but I have not tried to replicate his rhyming. The same can be said for meter. Given that Arabic metrical feet are quite different from Western ones, I have not stuck to any metrical pattern, even when the poems are metrically composed. All the poems as rendered in English are free verse but with an attention to rhythm, musicality, and compression that I hope will please both the eyes and ears of English-language poetry readers.

This project could not have taken place without the help and encouragement of several friends and fellow poets. I am grateful to Larry Goldstein, Elisa McCool, Jessica Young, Alana Di Riggi, Tung-Hui Hu, Catherine Calabro, Rasheeda Plenty, Sarah Schaff, Elizabeth Gramm, Lauren Proux, and Charlotte Boulay for their incisive feedback on several sections of the book. Thanks also to Suhail Eshdoud for his assistance with especially difficult phrases. I am grateful to Shawkat Toorwa, Adnan Haydar, Michael Beard, and Alan Hibbard for the suggestiveness of their translations, which have informed mine. Finally, I would like to thank Adonis for entrusting me with this task, for making his time available to me, and for granting me the freedom to rove among the splendors of his work to choose among them. I hope that he and those familiar with his work find this volume a fair and judicious representation of his work.

ACKNOWLEDGMENTS

Some poems published here previously appeared in the following publications:

Bat City Review: "This Is My Name" (excerpt).

Diode: "Home," "Love," "To a Soothsayer," "Song."

Green Mountains Review: "The Poets," "The Experiment," "Prodigal," "The Beginning of Poetry," "The Beginning of Sex," "The Beginning of Encounter," "The Beginning of Sex II," "The Beginning of Death."

Guernica: "A Mirror for the Twentieth Century."

The Kenyon Review: "Desert."

The New Yorker: "West and East," "Celebrating Childhood," "The Beginning of Speech," "A Mirror for a Question."

Pleiades: "Tree of Winding Curves," "Morning Tree," "Tree ['I have not carried . . .']," and "Tree ['He does not know . . .']."

PEN International: "I Imagine a Poet."

SubTropics: "The Wound."

Two Lines: "The Beginning of Doubt," "The Beginning of Love," and "The Beginning of the Road."

World Literature Today: "Season of Tears."

First Poems

1957

LOVE

The road and the house love me,
the living and the dead,
and a red clay jug at home
loved by water.

The neighbor loves me,
the field, threshing floor, and fire.

Toiling arms that better
the world, love me,

and go unrewarded with joy.

And tatters of my brother scattered about,
torn from his wilted chest
hidden by wheat spikes and season,
a carnelian from which blood shies.

He was the god of love as long as I lived.
What will love do if I too am gone?

SECRETS

Death holds us in its embrace,
reckless and modest,
carries us, a secret with his secrets
and turns our multitudes into one.

ELEGIES (for my Father)

1.

My father is a tomorrow
that floats down toward us,
a sun,
and above our house clouds rise.

I love him, a difficult buried secret,
a forehead covered with dirt.

I love him, his decaying bones and mud.

2.

Above our house silence heaved,

                       and a quiet weeping ascended—
and when my father fell to death
a field dried out, a sparrow fled.

THEY SAY I'M DONE FOR

They say I'm done for
and nothing remains of my joy
no oil, no flame.
I walk past roses, and what do they
care if I laugh or weep?
In roses, inside my eyes
and in my soul, there is a morning
in which I erase and am erased.
I love, I love beauty
and in it I worship my follies,
the ones I found on my own,
and the ones to which I was led.

You've become thirsty—
when will you say,
"I'm sated," my blood.
I thirst for an hour
for which I would bet all my days.
I thirst for a deep, open heart.
I'll light its flame along my road
store it among my veins
somewhere between alive and dead.
You've become thirsty—

when will you say
"I'm sated," my youth, my blood.

They say I'm done for
even as the earth's glory stands before me,
her largesse.
Her hands wound me
and her chest worships me.
And when her thorns heal me
her roses capture me again.

They say I'm done for
as the ages hold me dear,
and become drunk
at the mention of my name.
They say I'm done for
while on every path
a thousand hearts greet me,
shadows and houses laugh.
I drink to every heart,
I drink until rapture.
I say, soul, you are released,
become now what you always wished.

HOME

The story of ghosts in our house,
a horizon that crosses our lips
hidden by plow and threshing floor.

In it
we are lit by our distant journeys,
our dreams of the unknown.

From it
we leap from one universe to another,
and fly one generation after the next.

THE BANISHED

On the first day of the year
our groans said to us,
"Tie the ropes of travel and aim far
or live in tents of snow.
Your country is no longer here."
We who rebelled against the intruder
who were destroyed and banished—
emptiness now feeds on our cries,
ahead now walks behind us
and our days are frozen on our limbs,
cramped like our blood.
They have begun to live on seconds
to spin without time.

Banished, lost among the roads
a cipher to arms and heart,
hunger is all our cries
and the wind our clothes.
Even the morning flees from our sight,
glares hatred into our eyes.

Stay here, our hearts, do not leave us,
do not dare your fate

among hunger and bitter despair.
Stay here on this soil and grow
and tomorrow it will be said
from this earth a struggle arose,
fed on our arms,
nourished by our call,
an endless search
for a new dawn.

RAINS

He holds the plow to his chest,
clouds and rain in his palms.
His plow opens doors
toward a richer possibility.
He scatters dawn on his field
and gives it meaning.

Yesterday we saw him.
On his path there was
a geyser of daylight's sweat
that returned to rest in his chest,
clouds and rain in his palms.

A COAT

In our house there is a coat
that my father's life had stitched
with threads of fatigue.
It tells me—you sat on his rug
like a cut-off branch
and in his mind you were
tomorrow's tomorrow.

In our house there is a coat
tossed somewhere, uncared for,
that binds me to this ceiling
to this mortar and stone.
In its holes I see
my father's embracing arms,
his heart, and a yearning
housed deep within.

It guards me, wraps me,
lines my road with prayers,
entrusts his flute reed to me,
a forest and a song

TO A SOOTHSAYER

Her eyebrows are bells that ring
my unknown fate,
my now and my apprehension,
and all that I have been.

She looks and the signs
light up like lanterns
as if she'd clung
to time's eyelashes.
In morning
or under cloud or wind,
in ease or in distress,
she carries the knot of every epoch.

She holds my fingers and stares
and ponders,
rummages through caves,
unearths alphabets.

Won't you laugh, won't you frown?
Won't you whisper?
This is my hand, take it,
take my tomorrow.

Divine, improvise
and whisper, but beware
not to speak out loud.

LABOR PAINS

For whom does dawn open my eye's window,
for whom does it blaze a path between my ribs?

Why does death pulse through me
and tie my life to the flutter of seconds?

I've known my blood to be time's womb,
and that on my lips quake the labors of truth.

OBSCURE DISTANCES

Whenever my hands gather her things
       and bend like wheat stalks,
       like a horizon unharvested,
a light passes through me silken-stepped,
       its path studded with thorns,
and silence begins to call out my name.

My house and I in midmorning light,
       a flower grown old
       and a dead swallow's beak.

LONGING

I have a longing other than longing,
other than what fills the chests of the years.
Things approach it as if
they know no other destination.
They say: Without it we would not have become.

As if it is greater than itself,
this longing rises, extends, and is never satisfied.
It wishes to release itself from itself
and to fasten sky to earth.

A PRIESTESS

Around my forehead, a priestess burned
her incense and began to dream
as if her eyelids were stars.

Seer of generations, tell us
something about a god who is born.
Tell us:
Is there anything to be worshipped in his eyes?

SONG

from "Elegy for the First Century"

Bells on our eyelashes
and the death throes of words,
and I among fields of speech,
a knight on a horse made of dirt.
My lungs are my poetry, my eyes a book,
and I, under the skin of words,
on the beaming banks of foam,
a poet who sang and died
leaving this singed elegy
before the faces of poets,
for birds at the edge of sky.

Songs of Mihyar of Damascus

1961

PSALM

He comes bereft like a forest and like clouds, irrefutable. Yesterday he carried a continent and moved the sea from its place.

He draws the unseen side of day, kindles daylight in his footsteps, borrows the shoes of night, and waits for what never comes. He is the physics of things. He knows them and gives them names he never reveals. He is reality and its opposite, life and its other.

When stone becomes a lake and shadow a city, he comes alive, alive and eludes despair, erasing a clearing for hope to dwell, and dancing so the dirt will yawn, and trees fall asleep.

Here he is announcing the lines of peripheries, etching a sign of magic on the brow of our age.

He fills life and no one sees him. He shapes life into foam and dives. He turns tomorrow into prey and chases desperately after it. His words are chiseled on the compass of loss, loss, loss.

Bewilderment is his country, though he is studded with eyes.
He terrorizes and rejuvenates.
He drips shock and overflows with ridicule.
He peels the human being like an onion.

He is the wind that never retreats, water that never returns to its source. He creates a race that begins with him. He has no offspring, no roots to his steps.
He walks the abyss, tall as the wind.

NOT A STAR

Not a star, not a prophet's inspiration
not a pious face worshipping the moon,
here he comes like a pagan spear
invading the land of alphabets
bleeding, raising his hemorrhage to the sun.
Here he comes wearing the stone's nakedness
thrusting his prayers into caves.

Here he comes
embracing the weightless earth.

KING MIHYAR

King Mihyar
a sovereign, dream is his palace and his gardens of fire.
A voice once complained against him to words
and died.
King Mihyar
lives in the dominion of the wind
and rules over a land of secrets.

HIS VOICE

Mihyar, a face betrayed by his lovers,
Mihyar, bells that do not toll.
Mihyar written on the faces,
a song that visits us unawares,
on white, abandoned roads.
Mihyar, the castaway's bell
echoing on the hills of Galilee.

AN INVITATION TO DEATH

(Chorus)

Mihyar strikes at us.
He singes and chafes the skin of life
right off of us,
rids us of patience and soft features.

Surrender then to terror and tragedy,
land that wedded gods and tyrants,
surrender to his fire.

NEW COVENANT

He does not know how to speak these words.
He does not know the voice of the wilderness.
He is a priest who sleeps like a stone
weighed down with strange languages.

Here he is crawling under rubble
in the climate of new alphabets
offering his poems, rough and magical
like copper, to dejected winds.

He is a dialect that rolls in waves.
He is the knight of unfamiliar words.

THE END OF THE SKY

He dreams of tossing his eyes
into the well of the coming city,
dreams of dancing toward the abyss,
of forgetting his days that devour things,
days that create them,
dreams of rising, of collapsing
like the sea—forcing secrets to birth themselves,
starting a new sky at the end of the sky.

HE CARRIES IN HIS EYES

He carries in his eyes
a pearl; from the ends of days
and from the winds he takes
a spark; and from his hand,
from the islands of rain
a mountain, and creates dawn.
I know him—he carries in his eyes
the prophecy of the seas.
He named me history and the poem
that purifies a place.
I know him—he named me flood.

VOICE

He lands among oars and rocks,
encounters the lost
in jugs proffered to brides,
in the whispers of seashells.
He declares the birth of our roots,
our weddings, harbors, and singers.
He utters the rebirth of the seas.

THE WOUND

1.

The leaves asleep under the wind
are the wounds' ship,
and the ages collapsed on top of each other
are the wound's glory,
and the trees rising out of our eyelashes
are the wound's lake.
The wound is to be found on bridges
where the grave lengthens
and patience goes on to no end
between the shores of our love and death.
The wound is a sign,
and the wound is a crossing too.

2.

To the language choked by tolling bells
I offer the voice of the wound.
To the stone coming from afar
to the dried-up world crumbling to dust
to the time ferried on creaky sleighs
I light up the fire of the wound.
And when history burns inside my clothes
and when blue nails grow inside my books,

I cry out to the day,
"Who are you, who tosses you
into my virgin land?"
And inside my book and on my virgin land
I stare into a pair of eyes made of dust.
I hear someone saying,
"I am the wound that is born
and grows as your history grows."

3.
I named you cloud,
wound of the parting dove.
I named you book and quill
and here I begin the dialogue
between me and the ancient tongue
in the islands of tomes
in the archipelago of the ancient fall.
And here I teach these words
to the wind and the palms,
O wound of the parting dove.

4.
If I had a harbor in the land
of dream and mirrors, if I had a ship,
if I had the remains
of a city, if I had a city
in the land of children and weeping,
I would have written all this down for the wound's sake,

a song like a spear
that penetrates trees, stone, and sky,
soft like water
unbridled, startling like conquest.

5.
Rain down on our desert
O world adorned with dream and longing.
Pour down, and shake us, we, the palms of the wound,
tear out branches from trees that love the silence of the wound,
that lie awake staring at its pointed eyelashes and soft hands.

World adorned with dream and longing
world that falls on my brow
like the lash of a wound,
don't come close—the wound is closer—
don't tempt me—the wound is more beautiful.
That magic that your eyes had flung
on the last kingdoms—
the wound has passed over it,
passed and did not leave a single sail
to tempt toward salvation, did not leave
a single island behind.

SPELL

I see among the battered books
under the yellow dome
a punctured city flying.
I see walls made of silk sheets
and a murdered star
swimming in a green vessel.
I see a statue made of tears,
of the clay of limbs—and prostration
at the feet of a king.

THE FALL

I live between fire and plague
with my language, with these mute worlds.
I live in an apple orchard and a sky,
in the first happiness and the drollness
of life with Eve,
master of those cursed trees,
master of fruit.

I live between clouds and sparks,
in a stone that grows, in a book
that knows secrets, and knows the fall.

DIALOGUE

—"Who are you, who do you choose, Mihyar?
Wherever you went, to God or the Devil,
one abyss comes, another goes,
and the world is a choice."

—"I'll choose neither,
both are walls
both shutter my eyes.
Why would I replace one wall for another
when my sorrow belongs
to the one who brings light,
the sorrow of having known everything."

SEVEN DAYS

Mother who mocks
my love and contempt,
you too were made in seven days.
The waves were made then and the horizon,
and the feathers of song,
and my seven days were once wounded and estranged.
Why so unfair then
when I too am made of wind and dust?

A VISION

Mask yourself with burned wood,
Babel of fire and secrets.
I am waiting for the god who arrives
dressed in flames,
adorned with pearls stolen
from the lungs of the sea and from shells.
I am waiting for a god who loses his way,
who rages, weeps, bends, and shines.
Your face, Mihyar,
prophesies the god who will arrive.

WHAT TO LEAVE BEHIND

Go on, move, go and embrace the waves and the air
and lift with your eyelashes lightning and clouds.
Let them shatter
our mirror then, and the vessel of years.
And leave for us behind you—
No, no, leave nothing behind
except some sorrow and some mud
and the blood dried up in veins.

Ah, go on, move. No, wait, you're
not leaving, are you?
If so leave for us behind you
your eyes, your tawny corpse, your clothes,
a poem for the strange world,
the world borne of longing
holding in its eyelashes
your sky.

A BRIDGE OF TEARS

There is a bridge of tears that walks alongside me
and breaks apart under my eyelids.
There is under my porcelain skin,
a knight from childhood
who ties his horses to the shadows of branches
with ropes of wind.
And in a prophet's voice
to us he sings:
O wind
O childhood
O bridges of tears
broken under my eyelids!

I TOLD YOU

I told you I heard the seas
recite to me their poems. I heard
the bells tolling in shells.
I told you I sang
in Satan's wedding, in the feast of myth.
I told you I saw
in the rain of history,
in the luminousness of the horizon,
a nymph and a house.
Because I sail my own eye,
I told you I saw everything
in the first step of distance.

IT SHOULD SUFFICE

It should suffice you to see.
It should suffice to die away from here
to embrace the dust.

No silence in your eyes, no words,
as if you were smoke.
Your skin falls somewhere
and you stand somewhere else.
It should suffice to live lost,
defeated, mute like a nail.

You will not see God on human brows.
It should suffice you, Mihyar,
to keep the secret that he erased.

It should suffice you to see.
It should suffice you to die away from here.

LIGHTNING

Lightning bent low toward me,
wept and slept
in a forest of doubts
not knowing who I am
not knowing that I am the master of the dark.
Lightning bent low toward me,
wept and slept
in my hands
having looked into my eyes.

MY SHADOW AND THE EARTH'S

Come down toward me, sky, come rest
in my narrow grave,
on my wide brow,
and become faceless and without hands,
without a rattle in your throat, without a pulse.
Come down, draw your shape as two,
my shadow and the earth's.

THUNDERBOLT

Green thunderbolt,
my spouse in sun and madness,
stone has fallen on eyelids
and now you must redraw the map of things.

I came to you from an earth without sky
filled with God and the abyss,
winged with eagles and gales,
barraging, thrusting sand
into the caverns of seeds,
bowing to the coming clouds.

Redraw the map of things,
dear image of madness and sun,
my green thunderbolt.

A BLOOD OFFERING

In the caves of an ancient pain
when I loved the god
and loved the palace courtesans
where we lived—I and madness, my friend,
I was lost among the months
so I crossed the desert
and left the road behind.
In the name of a god writing his book
in the caves of an ancient pain
I raise this blaze
and sacrifice a fly.
In the name of the suns coming toward me
I begin this wake.

SCENE

(A dream)

As if a storm interrogating stone
a storm interrogating sky
interrogating things
as if history is being washed inside my eye
as if the days fall from my hands
as if like fruit . . .

DIALOGUE

"Where were you?
What is this light weeping from your eyes?
Where were you?
Show me, what did you write?"

I did not answer her. I did not speak a word
for I have torn my papers
for I could not find a single star
through the clouds of ink.

"What is this light weeping from your eyes?
Where were you?"

I did not answer her. Night was a Bedouin's
tent, the candles a tribe,
and I a thin sun
under which the earth changed its skin
and the lost one met his endless road.

PSALM

I toy with my nation.

I see its future glimpsed through the eyelashes of an ostrich. I toy with its history and days and fall on them like meteor and storm. On the other side of daylight I begin its history again.

A stranger to you, I reside on the other edge, a nation that belongs only to me. In sleep and in waking, I open a blossom and live inside it.

It's necessary that something else comes alive. This is why I open caves under my skin for lightning to charge, and I build nests for it to reside. It's necessary that I cross like thunder through sad lips parched like straw, through autumn and stone, between skin and pores, between thigh and thigh.

This is why I sing, "Come to me, shape that suits our dying."

This is why I scream and sing, "Who will let us mother this space, who is feeding death to us?"

I move toward myself and toward ruins. The hush of catastrophe overtakes me—I am too short to circle around the earth like a rope, and not sharp enough to pierce through the face of history.

You want me to be like you. You cook me in the cauldron of your prayers, you mix me with the soldier's soup and the king's spices, then pitch me as tent for your governor and raise my skull as his flag—

Ah, my death

Come what may, I am still heading toward you, running, running, running.

A distance the size of a mirage separates you from me.

I rouse the hyenas in you and I rouse the gods. I plant schism within you and enflame you with fever, then I teach you to travel without guides. I am a pole among your cardinal directions and a spring walking the earth. I am a trembling in your throats; your words are smeared with my blood.

You creep toward me like lizards as I am tied to your dirt. But nothing binds us and everything separates us. I'll burn alone and I'll pierce through you, a spear of light.

I cannot live with you, I cannot live but with you. You are tidal waves inside my senses; there is no escape from you. Go ahead scream, "the sea, the sea!" But be sure to hang above your thresholds beads made out of the sun.

Rip open my memory, search for my face under its words, search for my alphabet. When you see foam weaving my flesh and stone flowing in my blood, you will see me then.

Shielded as if inside a tree's trunk, present and ungraspable like air, I will never surrender to you.

I was born inside the folds of lilac, grew up on an orbit of lightning, and now live between light and grass. I storm and I waken, I gleam and cloud, I rain and snow. The hours are my language and daylight is my homeland.

(People are asleep and only when they die do they awaken) or as it has been said, "Never become conscious in your sleep, otherwise you will die." Or as it will be said . . .

You are dirt on my windowpanes, I must wipe you off. I am the morning coming down, the map that draws itself.

Still, there is a fever inside me that burns for you all night through

and I wait for you
in the shell of night by the shore
in the hum roaring from the depth of the sea
in the holes in the sky's cape
in linden and acacia
among pines and cedars
in the underbelly of the waves, in salt
I wait for you.

SPELL

You have no arteries.
Your skin, alive, spins around itself alone
and dives in a whirlpool of scales.
Your skin lives desiccated, naked,
your skin a rubber made of
living words wrapped on a house
of marble and sand.

Your decrepit days will come
in the pupa of a blind locust
reaching toward you dressed in spider skin.

FAREWELL

We bid you farewell years ago.
We wrote you a repentant elegy.
O halos of dead angels,
O language of rampaging locusts,
words are mired in mud,
words are adorned with labor pains.
Our missing wombs have returned,
and now come the rains and floods.
O language of ruins,
O halos of dead angels!

THE FLOOD

Fly on, dove, we don't want you to return.
They have surrendered their flesh to the rocks.
And I, here, am lurching toward an abysmal decision
clinging to the ark's sail.
Our flood is a planet that does not revolve,
decrepit and old.
Perhaps we'll catch in it a scent of the god of buried ages.
Fly on, dove, we don't want you to return.

ADAM

Adam whispered to me
choking on a sigh,
on silence and whimpers—
"I am not the world's father.
I never saw heaven.
Take me to God."

*Migrations and Transformations in the
Regions of Night and Day*

1965

FLOWER OF ALCHEMY

I must travel to a paradise of ashes,
walk among its hidden trees.
In ash, myths, diamonds, and golden fleece.

I must travel through hunger, through roses, toward harvest.
I must travel, must rest
under the bow of orphaned lips.

On orphaned lips, in their wounded shade
the flower of that old alchemy.

TREE OF THE EAST

I have become a mirror.
I have reflected everything.
In your fire I have changed the ritual of water and plant.
I have changed the shape of sound and call.

I have begun to see you as two,
you and this pearl swimming in my eye.
Water and I have become lovers.
I am born in the name of water
and water is born within me.
We have become twins.

TREE OF WINDING CURVES

In the fields of melancholy, on grass,
           I draw my rainbow days
breaking the surfaces of mirrors
between the noonday sun
and the water in Adam's pool.

My years float like hunger then descend
           to a forest of winding curves.
Years and years
I see their beaks entangle,
           then fall in a forest of winding curves
into their eternal nests.

TREE OF FIRE

A clan of leaves
throngs around a spring.
They scrape the land of tears
when they read fire's book
to the water below.

My clan did not wait for me.
They left,
no fire,
no trace.

MORNING TREE

Morning, come meet me—
toward our field—
on the road to our field.
Dried up trees, as I'd promised,
two beds as before, two children
in their dried-up shade.

Come meet me. Have you seen the boughs,
heard their call,
the sap their words leave behind?

Words that hold eyes in their grasp
words that pierce through stone.

Come meet me
come

as if we'd met before
woven the fabric of the dark
and dressed up in it, knocked on its door, lifted the curtain
opened its windows and lay
among the bends in the branches,

as if we'd sought the help of our eyelids and poured
the pitcher of tears and dreams,
as if we'd remained
in the land of boughs
and lost our way home.

TREE OF MELANCHOLY

Leaves tumble, then rest in the ditch of writing,
carrying the flower of melancholy
before speech becomes
echoes
copulating among the rinds of the dark.

Leaves wander and roll about seeking a land of enchantment,
forest after forest,
carrying the flower of melancholy.

SEASON OF TEARS

(a poem in the voice of Abdulrahman al-Dakhil, falcon of Quraish)[1]

It falls quiet, the call of the wilderness.
Clouds traipse above the palms
and from the edge of the groves
the towers are tinted rose.
It falls quiet, the call of return.

I ask her, and Damascus does not answer
does not come to the stranger's aid.
> *Will he stop here if he passes by?*
> *He died without a sound.*
> *Without a secret to his name.*
I live where she sleeps, among her long exhales
in the weeping fields
in the bed spread by her tears
in the small hallway
between her eyelids and sky.

It falls quiet, the call of return.

Of my life, nothing remains in my eye
except these sad ghosts.
Still the trees that weep on the city's ground
are lovers who sing my songs.

Mirror of endless wandering,
change the face of the moon,
for my beloved's face is no longer there.

Yesterday, we climbed toward that star,
saw him in the nude,
saw him clothed
and what we saw struck us—
a face made of dirt.
Change the face of the moon,
now that her face is no longer there,
O mirror of endless loss.

It falls quiet, the call of return.

I walk and the Euphrates alongside me walks,
the trees follow like flags
and a pair of eyes from the embers of years.
I sway with the swaying waist of the beast.
I dance with a black star.

And the towers
are melodies displaced from their scores.

> *My body and its captors are in one land,*
> *my heart and its owners elsewhere.*

It falls the quiet, the song of return
and the towers are a country of tears.

> *If she'd only known, she'd have wept*
> *the Euphrates and its banks of palms.*

It falls quiet, the song of return.

Confused, confused, I own a choked language that raves, towers I own
confused, crucifying day, tempted by a terror in its depth, tempted to rage
confused, the shores rob my inheritance, the waves defend my dawn,

> *I sang of gardens and a towering palace*
> *while in wretchedness, in attics hid.*
> *Tell him who used to sleep on soft cushions*
> *that the heights are being punished by a star.*
> *Tell him to ride through the specter of hardship*
> *or he'll become the lowest of men.*

It falls quiet, the song of return.

Wronging myself, I roll my history, slit its throat
in my hand, rouse it back to life.
I shepherd my eras, torture my mornings.
I feed them night, and feed them mirage.
I have a shadow that fills my earth
and lengthens. It sees, and greens, it burns its past
and like me,

burns itself.

> And we live together, walk together, the same
> green language on our lips.
> And in the face of midmorning light
> and in the face of death
> our ways part.

It falls quiet, the song of return:

I dream of Damascus,
of terror in the shadow of Qassiyun,
a past era stripped of its eyes,
of a calcified body, wordless tombs
calling out, Damascus
die here and let your promises burn,
calling out, Damascus, die and never return,
you chased prey of fattened thighs,
woman offered to whomever comes your way,
to chance, to a daring wayfarer,
sleeping through fever and through ease
in the arms of the East.
I drew your eyes in my book.
I carried you, a debt on my youth
in the greenness of Ghota,[2] the foothills of Qassiyun,
woman of mud and sin
temptress made of light.
A city,
Damascus once your name.

Yesterday
poetry, daylight, and I
reached Ghota and stormed
the gate of hope
howling at trees,
howling at water and fields
weaving out of them an army and a flag
to raid your black sky,
and Damascus, our hands continue to weave.
Nothing, not even death, can dissuade us.
When will we die, Damascus,
when will we find ease?

And last night, in dream, Damascus,
I shaped a statue of clay.
In his white curves I planted
your history, Damascus,
and I began in terror and in joy
to fall like a quake
on the hill of Jilliq.[3]
I embraced her, stroked her and sang
mmm mmm crescent moon.
And I said, No, you'll remain in longing, Damascus
in my blood,
and I said, let Damascus burn,
and my murdered depths arose
calling out to Damascus,
their frightened cries.

Woman of disobedience, without certainty,
woman of acquiescence,
woman of hubbub and shock,
woman of veins filled with forests and swamp,
naked woman lost to her thighs
listening to the dead, to graves, to dens,
listening with pious ears,
in love with your yellow corpses, your victims
feeding on mud and tears.
City all eaten up, Damascus, feeding on skin and hide.

O love . . .
No,
O Damascus
if it were not for you
I would not have fallen into these gorges,
would not have torn down these walls
would not have known this fire that calls out,
that thuds our history and illuminates,
vessel of the world coming our way.

Pardon me, Damascus,
you sinner beatified by your sins.

TREE

The hungry plant
a forest for hope.
The sound of weeping rises
to the trees, and the branches become
a country for pregnant women,
a country for harvest.

Each branch is a fetus
that sleeps on a bed in the air
green, calling out enchanting cries
that had escaped the forest of ash
and the towers of catastrophe,
carrying the hungry's groans
seeking nature's sustenance.

TREE

Every day
behind the chapels, a child dies
planting his face in corners,
a ghost before whom houses run fleeing.

Every day
a sad apparition arrives from a grave
returning from the farthest reaches to a land of bitterness.
He visits the city, its squares and lounges
melting like lead.

Every day
from poverty, the ghost of the hungry arrives,
on her face a sign:
a flower or a dove.

TREE

He does not know how to beautify
                    swords with severed limbs.
He does not know how to make
                    his canines shine and glare.
They come after him from a river of skulls and blood
and they climb the short wall
and he is behind the door
                    (he dreams of remaining like a child behind the door)
reading the last book of the starved.

TREE

I told you: Wake up! I saw water
as a child shepherding wind and stone.
And I said: Under the water and fruit,
under the surface of wheat grains
there is a whispering that dreams
of being a song for the wound
in the dominion of hunger and weeping . . .

Wake up, I call out to you. Don't you recognize the voice?
I am your brother, al-Khidr.[4]
Saddle up the mare of death,
tear time's door off its frame.

TREE

I have not carried a spear, or gored
a head,
and in summer, and in winter
I migrate like a sparrow
into the river of hunger, into its magical watershed.

My kingdom wears the face of water.
I rule absence.
I rule in surprise and pain,
in clear skies and in storm.

No difference if I come near or move away.
My kingdom is in light
and the earth is my house door.

TREE

In Jeirun⁵ there is a door made of roses.
Passersby bathe in its scent.
There is a tent for wounds,
there is a forest for the morning,
its branches are bridges that eyes track
toward the wind's ferry
leading to another morning.
Nights are houses where the tired rest.
They spike their flutes and read
the books of water and dust.
They turn their trusted tears into
beads and laurel garlands,
necklaces, and a wound of roses in whose streams
passersby bathe.

TREE

He was wrapped with basil leaves,
with transparent angst and a clear conscience,
wrapped in silence
and a luminous tearing.
It was said that after the grave
he split open the grave, tossed his death and flew
searching for motherhood
on the earth of man.
And it was said his wife was poor.
Here behind that tiny hill,
pregnant
and in between day and night
in silence
in luminous tearing
she waits for the child who will arrive.

Stage and Mirrors

1968

A WOMAN AND A MAN

—Who are you?

—a mad mystic without a home

a stone fallen from sky, demon-bred

—Who are you?

Did you travel in my body?

—Many times

—What did you see?

—I saw my death

—Did you wear my face?

and saw my sun as shadow

and saw my shadow as a sun

and slid under my bed and revealed me?

—Did you reveal me?

—And now that we reflected each other, have you found certainty?

—No

—Were you healed by me, and remained afraid?

—No

—Do you know me now?

—Do you know me?

MAN'S SONG

Sideways,
I glimpsed your face drawn on the trunk of a palm
and saw the sun, black in your hands.
I tied my longing to that tree and carried night in a basket
                                  carried the whole city
and scattered myself before your eyes.
                 Then I saw your face hungry like a child's.
I circled it with invocations
and above it I sprinkled jasmine buds.

WOMAN'S SONG

Sideways,
I caught sight of his old man's face
robbed by days and sorrows.
He came to me holding his green jars to his chest
rushing to the last supper.
Each jar was a bay
and a wedding held for a harbor and a boat
where days and shores drown
where seagulls probe their past and sailors divine the future.
He came to me hungry and I stretched my love toward him,
a loaf of bread, a glass cup, and a bed.
I opened the doors to wind and sun
and shared with him the last supper.

THE HUNGRY ONE

He draws hunger in his book—
stars and roads—
and covers the page
with kerchiefs made of wind.
   And we see
   a loving sun flicking its eyelids
   and we see dusk.

RAGE

The Euphrates rages,
daggers rising from its banks,
towers of quaking earth and thunder,
and the waves are fortresses.

I see dawn, its wings clipped,
and water, its floods sharpened, embracing its spears.

The Euphrates rages.
No fire to extinguish this wounded rage. No prayer.

FOUR SONGS FOR TAMORLANE

A Mirror for Law
Shock and shake
the virgin's body
and the pregnant woman's . . .
Shock and tear asunder.
Leave no old man or child . . .
This is my law.

Conquest
A sparrow burns
and horses and women and sidewalks
are split like loaves
in Tamorlane's hands.

They
They came,
entered the house naked.
They dug,
buried the children
and left.

Flood

Mihyar sang tenderly, absolved, prayed, and accused.
He blessed the face of madness,
melted the wound of the ages
in his throat and longed
for his voice to be
a flood, and it became.

A MIRROR FOR A TYRANT

Spike of wheat by spike of wheat,
do not leave a single grain behind.
This harvest
is our paradise restored
our nation retrieved.

Tear the hearts before the chests
pull out all the roots
change this soil that has
carried them,
erase the time that told their history
and erase the sky that bent toward them.

Spike of wheat by spike of wheat,
so the earth will fulfill her covenant
spike of wheat by spike of wheat.

BULLET

A bullet spins
oiled with the eloquence of civilization.
It tears the face of dawn. No minute passes
       in which this scene is not replayed.
The audience
takes another gulp of life, and livens up.
No curtains drawn
no shadows, no intermission:
       The scene is history,
       the lead actor, civilization.

TWO POETS

Between echo and sound two poets stand.
The first speaks like a broken
moon
and the other is silent like a child
who sleeps every night cradled in
a volcano's hands.

A MIRROR FOR A DREAM

Take my dream,
sew it, wear it,
a dress.

>   You made yesterday
>   sleep in my hands,
>   leading me around,
>   spinning me like a moan
>   in the sun's carts,
>   a seagull soaring,
>   launched from my eyes.

A MIRROR FOR A QUESTION

I asked, and they said, the branch
swathed in flame is a sparrow.
They told me my face
was the waves, the world's face a pile of mirrors,
a lighthouse, and the sailor's sorrow.

I arrived and the world in my way
was ink, each gesture, a phrase.
I did not know that between it and me
there was a bridge named "Brotherhood"
made of steps, prophecy and fire.

I did not know that my face
was a ship that sails inside a spark.

A MIRROR FOR THE TWENTIETH CENTURY

A coffin that wears the face of a child,
a book
written inside the guts of a crow,
a beast trudging forward holding a flower,
a stone
breathing inside the lungs of a madman.
This is it.
This is the twentieth century.

A MIRROR FOR CLOUDS

Wings
but made of wax
and the falling rain is not rain
but ships that sail our weeping.

A MIRROR FOR KHALIDA

Wave
Khalida
is a sadness
that leafs the branches
                    around it,
Khalida
            a journey that drowns the day
            in the waters of eyes,
            a wave that taught me
            that the light of the stars
            the faces of the clouds
            and the moaning of dust
            are a single flower.

Under Water
We slept in sheets woven
out of night shade—Night was oblivion
and our insides sang their blood
to the rhythm of castanets and cymbals
to suns shining under water.
Night became pregnant then.

Loss

Once, I was lost in your hands, and my lips
were a fortress longing for a strange conquest
        in love with being besieged.
I moved forward
and your waist was a queen
and your hands were the army's commanders
and your eyes were a shelter and a friend.
We welded to each other, got lost together, we entered
the forest of fire—I drew the first step to it
       and you blazed a trail . . .

Fatigue

The old fatigue around the house
now has flowerpots and a balcony
where he sleeps. He disappears
and we worry about him in his travels, we run
circling the house
asking each blade of grass: we pray,
we catch a glimpse of it: We cry out: "What and where? All the winds
have blown
and every
branch shook with them,
but you did not come."

Death

After these seconds
the small time will return
and the steps and the pathways that had been trod.
Afterwards the houses will grow ancient
the bed will put out
the fire of its day and die
and the pillow will die as well.

THE MARTYR

When I saw night in his swollen eyelids
and found in his face
no date palms
no stars,
I stormed around his head
like the wind
and broke like a reed.

A MIRROR FOR BEIRUT

1.

The street is a woman
who reads *Al-Fatiha*[1] when sad,
or draws a cross.
Night under her breast
is a strange hunchback
who fills his sack
with silver howling dogs
and extinguished stars.

The street is a woman
who bites any who go past,
and the camel asleep by her breast
sings
to petroleum (each passerby singing past),
and the street a woman
in whose bed fall
days and vermin
and even man.

2.

Flowers painted on shoes
and the earth and sky
a box of colors—
and in cellars
history lies like a coffin.
In the moans of a star or a dying slave girl
men, women, and children lie
without blankets
or clothes.

3.

A cemetery:
a navel above a belt
made of gold,
and a poppy-like woman sleeps—
a prince and a dagger
doze on her breast.

A MIRROR FOR THE LOVER'S BODY

Each day the lover's body
melts in the air, becomes a scent
swirling, evoking every perfume.
He comes to his bed
covers
his dreams, dissolves like frankincense,
gathers like frankincense.
His first poems are a child in pain
lost in a labyrinth of bridges.
He does not know how to live in their water,
and does not know how to cross.

A MIRROR FOR THE HUSSEIN MOSQUE

Do you not see the trees hunchbacked
half-drunk, walking
slowly
to perform their prayers?
Do you not see an unsheathed sword,
and an armless executioner
bawling
and circling the Hussein Mosque?

WEST AND EAST

Everything stretches in history's tunnel.
Everything decorated is mined,
carrying its oily, poisoned child
sung to in a poisonous trade.
It was East, like a child asking,
          pleading
and West was his flawless elder.

I turn this map around,
for the world is all burned up:
East and West, a heap
of ash gathered
in the self-same grave.

A Time Between Ashes and Roses

1971

THIS IS MY NAME

Erasing all wisdom   this is my fire
   No sign has remained—My blood is the sign
                This is my beginning
   I entered your pool   Earth revolving around me, your organs are a Nile
flowing   We drifted   settled   You split through my blood and my waves
traversed your chest,   you melted so that we begin: Love has forgotten the blade-edge
of night   Shall I cry out that the flood is coming? Let's begin: A scream
scales the city and the people are mirrors on the march   When salt crosses over
toward . . . we'll meet   Will you be who you are?
—My love is a wound
   My body a rose on the wound, unpluckable except in death   My blood is a bough
that gave away its leaves and lay down to rest . . .

       Is stone the answer? Does your death, that sleeping master, beguile you? I have
halos of craving for your breasts, and for your childlike face, a face like it . . . You? I did
not find you

       It's my flame that erases now

       I entered your pool   I bear a city under my sorrows
I have what turns the green branches into snakes, and the sun into a black lover
I have

       Come closer, wretched of the earth, cover this age with your rags and tears,
cover it with a body seeking its own warmth   The city is arcs of madness
I saw revolution bear its own children   I buried millions of songs and I came
(Are you in my grave?) Let me touch your hands: Follow me

My time has yet to come, but the graveyard of the world is already here   I bear
ashes for all the sultans   Give me your hands Follow me

I can transform: Landmine of civilization—This is my name (a billboard)

The footsteps of life ended at the door of a book I erased with my questions
What do I see? I see sheets of paper where it is said, "Here civilization came to rest" (Do
you know a fire that weeps?) I see a hundred as two   I see mosque and church
as two executioners and the earth a rose

An eagle flies toward my face   I sanctify the scent of chaos
so that a sad time will come for the people of flame and refusal to rise
My desert grows   I loved a befuddled willow, a bridge that gets lost, a minaret
that suffers old age   I loved a street where Lebanon set its entrails in rows, in pictures,
mirrors and amulets

I said, I will give myself to the abyss of sex and allow fire to conquer
the world   I said, stand like a spear, Nero, in the forehead of creation   Rome
is all houses, Rome is imagination and reality   Rome city of God and history, I said,
stand like a spear, Nero

I had nothing to eat tonight except sand, my hunger spun like the earth   Stone,
palaces, temples   I pronounce them like bread   In my third blood I saw the
eyes of a traveler who soaked people in his eternal dream,
carrying the torch of distances inside the mind of a prophet and into savage blood

❀

And Ali, they threw him into a well and covered him with straw as the sun carried
her victims and left   Will light find its way to
Ali's land? Will it meet us? We heard blood and saw moaning

We will say the truth: This country
                raised its thighs
                as its flag

We will say the truth: This is not a country
                but our stable on the moon,
                the sultans' staff, the prophet's prayer rug

We will speak plainly: There is something called presence in the world,
                and something called
                absence   Let's tell the truth:
                We are absence
                The sky did not birth us, neither did dust
We are foam spewing from a river of words
Rust in the sky and its planets,
                rust in life
                (a secret manifesto)

My country is a refugee inside of me

Let my face become a shadow
     An eternity of enamored rocks circles me, for I am fire's first lover
     And fire is pregnant with my days, a rattle ringing on her breast
Her armpit is a well of tears, a lost river   The sun clings to her like a dress,
then falls   A wound she deepened into tributaries with vigor and spices
(Is this your fetus?)   My sadness is a rose
     I entered the school of grass, my forehead cracked, and my blood stripped of
strength:
     I asked, what should I do   Should I ring the city with a belt of bread?   I scattered
myself in fire's colonnades   We divided the blood of kings and we hungered
We carried the epochs
mixing pebbles and stars
driving clouds
like a herd of fortresses

I can transform: Landmine of civilization—this is my name

The nation rested
in the honey of sanctuary and violin
The creator fortified it like a trench
     and barricaded it

No one knows where the door is
No one asks where the door is
        (a secret manifesto)

   And Ali, they threw him into a well   Embers were his shirt   We burned
and gathered his remains   I burned: Good evening, rose of ash!
Ali is a land whose name is without a language hemorrhaging oblivion
that binds grass with water   Ali is an immigrant

   Where does the master of sadness sleep, where does he carry his eyes? My sky is
        choked,
my shoulder falls, and the earth is a helmet filled with sand and straw   Terrified, I ran;
a swallow shelters me   I rose, her breasts are flames   I rose, opened a window:
Green fields   I am the other conqueror   The earth is a game   A mare totters into the clouds
The besotted trees emerge   A branch shakes me awake   Water gushes out   The old epochs
end and I begin   My face is made of orbits   There is a revolution inside the light

   A village awakens me inside the wind's well   Silence breaks apart
Embrace me,   maker of fatigue, offer me your pendulum   I am
rock, quest and question   There is no fire, no festival   I am the specter, standing guard
at the edge of the city while its people sleep   I fell into light's trap
pure like violence, luminous, and weightless like loss   My limbs are lightning, sculpted
winds   My bones do not taste of crown and silver   I am not a thing to be owned   My
        blood is the sky's migration,
my eyes are birds   They say your skin is made of thorns   Die then and let
my sky reflect your yellow skins   They say your skin is an eternity, sludge found at
        the bottom of a dream

Let the spears of endless war be born
There is a hole of devastation between us, and my voice
is the ravings of a warrior as he breaks the crutches of song and roots out the
          alphabet

      And the women gathered in the temple courtyard
      invoking the alphabets of holy books
      turning the sky
      into a doll
      or a guillotine
      and Ali shared his sorrows
      with the devotees of misery
      who became like eagles
      and were torn apart

      And Ali is a flame
      a magician that burns in all waters—
      storming he rages, invades all books and soils
      He sweeps away history and blots out
      the day with his wings
      It pleases him that the day
      had gone mad

      This is the time of death, but
      in each death there is an Arab death
      Days tumble into its squares
      like hacked branches of cedar

They were the last song heard
from a bird leaving a burning forest

❁

My country runs behind me like a river of blood   The forehead of civilization
is a floor slathered with algae   I gathered up a crown, I became a lamp   Damascus
went adrift, Baghdad fell to yearning   The sword of history is broken on the face of my
                country
    Who is fire? Who is flood?
I was desert when I held the ice within you and like you I broke into sand
and fog   I cried out, You are a god whose face I must see to erase what unites it
and me   I said, my "I" embodies you, you crater filled with my waves   I am night,
and you were barefoot when I tucked you into my navel   Within my steps you
                procreated a way
You entered my infant water   Light up, root yourself in my labyrinth

    A fruitful numbness grows around my head, a dream under a pillow   My days
are a hole in my pocket   The world has gone haggard   Eve is pregnant and wears
                my trousers
                                                  I walk on the ice of
my pleasures   I walk between miracle and confusion   I walk inside a rose

The flowers of despair wilt, sadness rusts   an army of pulverized
faces crossing history, an army like a thin thread that begged for peace and surrendered,
                an army like a shadow
I run inside the cries of the victims alone on the lip
of death like a grave moving inside a ball of light
    We melted into each other—the blood of our loved ones tender and protective

like an eyelid   I heard your pulse inside
my skin (Are you a forest?)   The barrier fell (Are you a barrier?)
the seagulls asked a thread woven by sailors,   and the ice of travel sang
a sun it cannot see (Are you my sun?)   My sun is a feather that drinks
the horizon   The lost one heard a voice (Are you my voice?)   My voice is my time,
your tasty pulse   your breast my blackness   and all night is my whiteness
A cloud crept toward me and I surrendered my face to the flood
and fell lost among my ruins

❀

This is how I loved a tent:
I turned the sand and its eyelashes into
trees that rain
and the desert into a cloud
I said: This broken earthen jug
is a defeated nation   This space
is ash   These eyes
are holes   I said madness
is a planet hidden inside a tree

I will see a crow's face
in the features of my country   I will name this book
"shroud."

I will name this city "stinking corpse"
and name the trees of the Levant, "sad birds"
(a flower or song
may grow out of my naming)

I will name the desert moon "date palm"
and the earth may waken and return
as a child, or a child's dream

     Nothing sings my songs now
               The protestors will come
and light will arrive on its appointed hour

Nothing but madness remains

Ashes of the hearth,
is there for my history a child in your night?
The revolution's rage is the embers of a lover
and a woman's song
Is there for my history a child in your night?

The dust of legends is in the bones now   Need I seek shelter? Need the dust?
No place for me, no use in death   This is the dizziness
of a man who sees the corpse of the ages on his face and falls   No motion
He believes old age
is a nipple for infants

I can transform: Land mine of civilization—this is my name

     Go back to your cave   Histories are swarms of locusts   This history
rests on a whore's breast, gargles, heaves in the belly of a she-donkey, craves the

earth's rot,

and walks inside a maggot   Go back to your cave, cast down your eyes

I see a word—

All of us around it are mirage and mud   Imruulqais[1] could not shake it away, al-Ma'ari[2] was

its child, Junaid[3] crouched under it, al-Hallaj[4] and al-Niffari too[5]

Al-Mutannabi[6] said it was the voice and its echo   "You are a slave,

and it is your angel master"   The nation is tucked deep within it like a seed

Go back to your cave

What? Did they banish him or kill him?

They killed him   I will not talk about my friend, death: A countryside of yellow

flowers around me, but I will write about the last branch of the cedar

in my home, the flutter of the dove dragging the night's rug away from the dream, high

                as a tower

They killed him   I will not utter the names of witnesses or murderers, and I

                will not weep

I will weep a nation born mute, the swan hatching the blueness of shores weeping

But why weep over a child, or a poet? I will write the last shadow

our cedar cast, the flutter of the dove as she drags night's rug away from a dream high

                as a mountain

     His majesty, the caliph issues a law made of water   His people are broth, mud,

     and wan, wilted swords   His majesty's word is a crown studded with human eyes

     Is this city a holy verse? Are the women wearing pages of the holy book?

     I tucked my eyes into a tunnel that the hours had dug   I asked, are my people

          a river without a sound?

                                                                I sing

the language of the spear tip   I cry out, time is ruptured, its walls have fallen

into my guts   I vomit, no history left in me, no present
I am the sun's insomnia, abyss, sin, and motion   Wait for me,
rider of the clouds   What I own beguiles me, and the sun strikes my limbs   I live
in the horizon and in psalms   I am a branch seeking shelter: Listen, can you hear this
crying coming from the liver of the world?   Listen,   I hear death sounding
from my wrinkles   We hallucinated
        I raved so to die well   I chose two breasts and they became my rites

Is your skin
the fall, are your thighs a wound that I filled with the world's
healing?   Are you night's fissure in my skin? My axe is sharp and
I have become another stream, my banks overflow   You scoop me into your arms   An
        arc
My face is a flying ruckus divided by sound   Ask me   I answer
An oracle spoke   Its horses sought me, and the whispering died out   Do you or I have
anything to whisper?   A bridled fire, ships stranded in a pacified sea?
A seagull opened its eyes—close yours—it forgot that the opening
in its ruffled feathers is water and sparks   If only there was thunder, if only it knew,
if only it were in my hand

        Be still   This is a dome, and my house is the nozzle of a breast   I will go on
                digging
If I change, if dust changes, if fire becomes a glottal stop

❀

You melt into my sex, my sex without borders or swords   Annihilate yourself
And I annihilated myself   We are a single face, my shirt is not made of apples and you
        are not a paradise   We are

a field, a harvest, the sun stands on guard   I ripen you   Come to me from that
green edge there, this is our yield, our bodies, sower and reaper
Come to me, my limbs, along from that edge as I invoke
my death   Break me into a chain of epochs   The ember of time is our domain
    Longing is
        our domain   The riches of the universe
are ours as it dresses itself in humankind and as we discover a way

        I read in yellowed papers that I will die banished   The desert broke up into pieces
                of light,
and my people scattered   We scratched the earth for words that tasted
like virgins   Damascus enters my clothes, in dread, with love, shaking
my insides with raves and tremors

        You shed your skin   Let your lips be   Melt them between my teeth   I am night
and I am day   I am time   We have melted into each other   Root yourself into my
    labyrinth

                                    ✿

This is how I loved a tent
how I turned the sand in its eyelashes
into trees that rain
and the desert into a cloud
I saw God, a beggar on the land of Ali
I ate the sun on the land of Ali
baked the minarets like bread
I saw the sea raging out of the fog of smokestacks
whispering

"Whoever made us
made no more than a roofed shelter
Storms shook it and it fell and became
wood to be burned in the caliph's hearth"

The sea rarely speaks, but the sea
did speak: "We've become bone dry
and history has ground itself to death
in its repetition in the windmills"
The creator has fallen into his tomb
The creature has fallen into its tomb

And the women gather to rest
in the temple courtyard
luring night out of its wells
sewing the sky
and singing:
Ali is a fire
        a magician burning in every water
And they ask the sky:
Is it a star or mummy,
this earth?
Then they unthread the sky
and patch it up again

Dajjal[7] buried a people in his eyes
Dajjal excavated a people from his eyes
and we heard him praying above them

and we saw how he made them kneel
and we saw
how the people were like water cupped in his palms—
and we saw
how water became a windmill

Islands made of fire, Asia rises among them   Tomorrow rises,   and sunlight
goes out   We dream what did not happen at night   My day is measured
in fire   So I cry out   The voice of the masses conquers the universe and confuses

I am not ash or wind

My bed is tastier and further   Cages, abandoned pathways
and the horse of the past is all ash
and the color of God is another hue
                    No hand weighs me down

Ali, eternity of fire and childhood,   do you hear the lightning of the ages,
hear the sighs of their steps?   Is the road a book or a hand?   The fingers
of dust are like a dervish singing to a king in a legend   Bring the country, bring the
                cities near   Shake the tree of dreams, reshape the trees of
                sleep, and what the sky says to the earth:
        A child is lost under the navel of a black woman searching and lost
                A child whose hair grays
        and the earth's god is a blind man dying

Peace!

To the faces walking the solitude of the desert, to the East dressed in grass
and fire   Peace to Earth, washed by the sea, peace to its love
Your nakedness has unleashed its rains   It has stored thunder in my chest
and time leavens there   Come close   This is my blood, the brilliance of the East
   Scoop

        me up and disappear
Lose me   I hear the echo of thunder in your thighs   Cover me   Come and live inside
        me
My fire is direction, the planet is my wound, a gift I pronounce
And I pronounce a star, I draw it
escaping from my country to my country
I pronounce a star that my country draws
into the footsteps of its defeated days—
O ashes of the word
Is there a child for my history in your night?

Nothing but madness remains

I see him now out of the window of my house
sleepless among sleepless stones
like a child taught by a sorceress
that there is a woman in the sea
who carried his history inside a ring

and she will come
when the hearth fire dies out
and when night melts in sorrow
among the ashes of the hearth

And I saw history inscribed on a black flag shifting like a forest
                                        I did not write it down

I live in longing, in fire, in rebellion, in the magic of its crafty poison
My country is this spark, this lightning in the darkness of the time that remains

Singular in a Plural Form

1975

BODY

1.

The earth is not a wound
        but a body—   Can one travel between a wound
              and a body?
Can one reside?

      Physicians, herbalists, magicians, diviners
      readers of the unknown
I am working your secret trade
I become an ostrich = I swallow the embers of shock
           and grind the boulders of murder

I work your secret trade = I witness the unknowns of my state
      I pant like someone trying to make home of his exile
      I scatter—am diffused—my surfaces spread and I own none of them
      my insides reduced, no place in them for me to live
Then in an instant
      I dry up   I dew
      I move away   approach
      I retreat   attack
      I worship   shake off belief
Something separates me from me

How do I show myself to my body?

A *Piece of Bahlul's Sun*[1]

Two lips attack his thighs   they repeat
          a history that repeats itself
Who sees eternity now?
Who touches the beginning?
          E T E R N I T Y   =   B E G I N N I N G
Seduce him   pulse that rules the unknown
          become his rhythm
Offer his head to fall into your arms
He is the tried   the pure
He is eloquent water
He is the shape that streams semen and light

2.
His stay among trees and grass had the dark shiver of reeds and the drunkenness of
          wings
          He bonded with the waves
          He gently seduced the stones
          He convinced language to procure the ink of poppies

A ladder called "time" leaned on his name and ascended
                    prophecy by
                    prophecy →

From wings an ether streamed
from coincidence   to certainty

But
sun O sun what do you want from me?

      A face that gathers into lake   and breaks into swan
      A chest that shivers lark   and calms to lotus
      A pool that opens to rose   closes in pearl
These are the jungles of migration and the flags of poverty
The day has the hands of a toy
The heavens burble like a clown

But
sun O sun what do you want from me?

      Death wears the state of narcissus
      Narcissus inhabits bowls of ice   dreams that love is a face
         and he is its mirror
      Stones are blossoms, the clouds butterflies
and on the threshold a body—a spark with which to read the night
Death is not the body's desolation
      Death is the solitude of what is not a body
But
sun O sun what do you want from me?

Barricades multiply me
      Veils render me luminous

I breathe in the herbs of the depths
and between my feet there is nothing but cages

If the cage ignites and time is a jungle
if jungle is a woman
if the sky undoes its buttons
                    I will heal from "if" and "wish"
          to say, "rush out, sky, and find you
                    another motherhood
          release your eyelashes from tears
          surrender to another water"
I am not dream or eye
          No wisdom to me   My wisdom is that the wind bears the fruit
                    that feeds my days
that my days have ships that carry the shores

But
how to calm these ports that guard the waves
                              and you
sun O sun   what do you want from me?

          I seek what never meets me
          In its name I plant myself a rose for the winds
                              north south east west
          I add height and depth
but how to find my way?
          My eyes look like pieces of bread
and my body descends toward an illness that has the sweetness of a woman's down →

> Love cannot chase me
> and hatred cannot reach me

But
how do I find direction, and what do you want from me
sun O sun?

3.

He erases his face	he discovers his face
Rapture advances	A temptation wears you in her first dawn
Time advances	Where do you chronicle life and how?
Darkness advances	What tremor will spread you, woman, among my blood cells
	so that I'll say "you are climate, turn, and sphere"?
	What aftershock?
Light advances	It becomes night in my regions

> I am torn and assembled
> Time takes the shape of skin
> and escapes time

And your conquest
befell
me →

                                My metamorphoses heaved toward you—
When you entered,
            why did you take the burning fields even though my hands were the
                        first fire
and why, every night

did I carry the softness of your breasts to another night?

                                            Enter, woman,

                                            with dirt

on your knees, the dirt of the road that leads to you, to

mountains

and the cypresses of the mountainsides

and the larches of the valleys   I say we shall meet-separate

          and I will gather my regions:

       Bitter apples that scatter like salt on tables of licentiousness

          you are the sweetest, and I offer you the first taste of me

                           Enter

we meet-separate   Separation is not a wing, and meeting is not a shadow

I hide among the features of my face

you hide between your breasts—

          Mix us together, mountainsides

          a body bolting out

          a body taming

          Draw us

The book of ladders is now complete

the suitcases of migration are now open →

                 Your body is a loss I leave behind

                 and you are the books of my departure

I take you, a land I do not know

      hills and valleys covered with the herbs of seeking

mysterious stretches

and I take you standing

      sitting

lying

None but you convinces me

I take you

in my sighs
in waking   in sleep
in the states between
and in what time promises me

I take you

fold by fold
and I open my entries to you

I stretch within you and do not reach
I circle and do not reach
I stretch like wire, I thread myself into yarn
I rove your expanses and do not reach
You are beyond distances, beyond victories
You are Where and If, and What and How and When and you are
not you

Lie on my body, woman, and plant yourself

cell by cell
branch to branch
vein to vein

Let thousands of lips bloom from you
thousands of teeth
Let them be unknown, let them correspond to the measure of our love
This while

a limb is stupefied
a limb abducted
and in the folds of our hips and thighs a trickle covers you and covers me

and whose light goes out with each stroke

I would have hung your image by then

next to all the images

and revelation would have reached me and I would have said,

This is our last meeting →

Who are you?

I take you, man

angelic animal

who places poison on one lip

and balsam on another

and every night I say

this is our first meeting

singular man

m

o

l   u   m   i   n   o   u   s

n

Nothing between us except this call

these flashes of lightning

and all that floats

My body will shake with the divinity it demands

and the gifts it acquires

and I will cry out: You are dust

you are omnipotence

Who are you?

A body grows in lavender and lilac
it descends, it rises, it oversees
it gathers the banks and reads the mutterings of the reeds
      I spied you, woman, with my eyes
      a dance moving in steps with the season
      I sighed in spikenard
      I took shapes that came and went   In the tidal waves
of our waists one drowned body bumps into another
      I leave the bamboo thicket
I enter the pestle
I penetrate to the calyx
where the ovules rest and the pole of the stamen ends
      I gather myself   like pollen upon pollen
                I take you off
      I wear you
I skin myself off of you   I unite with you
      and between us I create
      a delusion as high as the sun
lies that break time branch by branch

      Who are you?

Under skin, your true self
and in my arteries a streak of madness
      I roll between the I of ember and the I of ice
      and between the "Ya"
      and the "Alif"
      I dangle

I create in day another day
and I tie my whims with a rope of minutes
The mirror says break me
the steps say tie me up
and between the machinery of death and the animal of pronunciation
      I plant myself   I root
and play nature's dice

A Piece of Bahlul's Sun

    You once said:
    Hire me to guard the coffers of your body and store me
    your body white lilies, my body a lake
And said:
You whose wide banks are sprawled on the horizon of our dominion
you   O ship →   take wing
      Maybe the mosses will flake off
      and the bedrock of our secret will blaze
There are caverns covered with rust—   take wing
        to where a wing's sway is the body's temple
        and the body is the priest of madness

And man, you once said:
hand in hand   heart on heart
body and wind walk → the storms do not cease

and the skin does not seek shelter
and the body maddens its way to sense
and the wind takes up the madness of oceans

And man, you said:
how do pebbles swim while cupped in hands
        how does water stream from fingers?
And said:
I will ask my time to release me so that I become a sign of what love will be
And said:
Love also wounds life → it uproots and banishes
The body also becomes a liquid and takes the shape of the vessel
And said:
It is the body, not love, that is the skin of time, the pores on the earth's hide
The body, not love, is the arc of the horizon and the wind's muscle

        You want to know?
        Stop knowing what you are
        and stop knowing others

And man, you said:
I mixed and bent
        I stole my voice, stripped my words
        and placed language in its sheath

And you cried,
        O man

you who were created ill
when will you heal?

4.

Enter, woman   my limbs have become wanton
for you   they grab and grope
I wished into you

          and anchored my elements →
Enter   We meet = separate   We erase = discover
                                                                      our faces
     We mix bread and wound to keep the earth intact under our words
     We sustain the courage to refuse so that we write another history
     We see a woman=lake   a river=lover's body
     our bodies levitate
     and rise into the heights

Naked
a celestial body leaves its home and descends our steps
Things murmur   a noise we bathe in
We befriend time's beasts
          We roam the countryside   we settle in cities
scatter   gird ourselves
We become familiar   we differ
Things do not have names
          things have thighs like stags
               and faces like lovers
               And here the horizon is →

                                                    white fur

Pillows exude the perfume of jungles
                         and here is the body-father   body-mother
                              heading to—
and we head to—
The bells of desire enliven us
beds high as childhood and truthful as the sun enliven us
and invent a death that lengthens life
and we invent a treachery
                    between you and me
                         a hypocrisy
                    that breaks time branch by branch
            We meet = separate = erase our faces = discover them
                    two silhouettes on the bed
one seeking to be seen   one hiding
and the two bodies are four
            half for the absent ones
            half for the present

                         A throng of needles strikes our bodies
                         and the body on whose door we knock does not shelter us
                         There are cracks that reveal what was covered
                         There are furrows and grooves that recite the world's first secrets
                              to us
How can one body flower into jasmine and boxthorn?
How can one heart dress itself in two bodies?

We join   =   we differ
We create treachery as high as childhood
            a hypocrisy honest as the sun
                        we invent a death that lengthens life
and say
love is three: man and man and woman
            man and woman and woman

                  There
                  is
                  always
                  a distance
                        between us   → we said
It is erased by a fire we call love
Day attaches itself to day and night attaches itself to night and a distance remains
            between us
We put out what is not extinguishable
We light what is not lightable
                  and a distance remains between us
and in the hours of joining heave and heave, droplet to drop
                  a distance remains between us
            O Love, extinguished species,
                  come and sit on my-knee/her-knee
            take the needles of tears and weave the water
The bells of desire enliven us
We invent a day that lengthens life
we invent a treachery that rises toward childhood

a hypocrisy honest as the sun

Who are we?

A bridge unites us that we cannot cross

a wall unites us, separates us   I enter you exit myself

I exit you enter me →

What I build tears me down

and you appear as space itself

and I, vision's vision

I held a rose   walked down into your valley and waited

A river between us and the bridge between us is another river

I heard you asking: Which of us is the liver

Which of us is the wailing

I mixed myself with impatience   rolled in its fragile nests

I cried out, we are one, a ball of fire

Put yourself out, woman   Put yourself out, man

so that we know the grace of embers

We erase our faces   we discover our faces

premonitions

shells

mirrors

Through them we cross to our other selves

We open our chests to the highest among them

and the lowest open us

and each of us enters the tower of aloneness

in the solitude of a bird dying

and each of us tastes the other

and his organs are drunk on life while the other's are drunk on death
and each of us denies YES while confessing NO
and denies NO while confessing YES

                     How do you wash your body, woman
while your other water disappears?

                     How do I wash my body and make my first water return?

I am your question
and you are not my answer
I knew you with my longing
I tied it to you   and welded you with my being

              A   I

                            L
              A   D   N   I   S
                            O

So that your body moves wisely
so that I move with it
       with what is above it
       below it
       and in between
so that I surround you and break any barrier that separates you from me
       I read the book of your priests
       I grow into your origins
       I taste their creatures   and personify them in my delusions
so that you become the dot
       and I become the script and shape
so that you become "From" and what follows it

"about" and what it possesses
                    where words cannot contain me
                    where only imaginings and symbols can contain me
                                        I did not intend you

I am not your sea
I am not the swans you wait for
I have nothing but limbs
            limbs that get lost   lost in a fever whose outer reaches I have yet to
                                                            discover

        After
I erased-discovered you
                    I spread my wings on leaves and invited you
I said, death is an old man
        how can he still chase us?
I said, my body is north and time is south
        how could they ever meet?
        For you are all that is before me and that cannot grow old
        for you are the eternity of the directions that remain in my limbs
        and you my eyes of insomnia and my sleep of despair
        and for your sake I have equated desert and sea
                    eye and thorn
        and for you I have plucked meaning from crowds of words and named him
                    "image"
        and in honor of your names which I sent down by decree
I told the alphabet that I longed for you and craved you
            and for you I have changed, and convinced my years to be the ember of change
            and for you I have bestowed errors to fire and convinced the body
                    to become the glory of all adjectives

I devour you cell by cell   and you do not sate me
I contain you heartbeat by heartbeat   and there's no comfort from you
                    Neither jealousy separates you from me   nor hatred
                    only a feeling that has no name
And now that you are time and death
how can I retrieve you?

You breathe your last   → I rush toward you
                    I seek the pulse of your traces
                    and touch your departure

                    I

                    never was

I am but a mist of desire
          I was the slow one and my clothes went past me
          My death is a ladder for my body, and my body is indecisive → where shall I rest
          I have affixed the clouds   I commanded foam to become
                              the key to the waves → Where shall I rest?
A name is not a root, a root is not a woman, is not → where shall I rest?
Straw is dressed in roses and words break their crosses → where shall I rest?

The horizon came to me   named itself after me
                    a name is not an embrace
                    an embrace is not a woman
                    I take my lips away from you tonight
you lustful earth that never ovulates
                    So that I know how you, desert, fall like rain

       how you expand
    so that I know the seal of despair
so that I know how we love when we do not love
    how what bore our first name wilts
        so that I quench my thirst with what we thought will never know wilting

Memory-forgetfulness
Wherever narcissus follows me   I follow the blueness
    I read your body
    its guests and subjects

And I say a fog rises out of my face
threads stream out of my body
    They knot and unravel and unravel
I ask someone who saw pebbled earth expand
and call out—

      Spread on, fire
      Guts, dry up and shrivel
         spread
      as coldness punishes muscles
         spread
      as time softens, softens
      as exhaled breaths swirl into halos and halos

The good road is not good for me
    and my steps belong to no one
    In each dot on my body is a false clue →

A rib is not a lover, a sign that misleads the roads

and woman is not earth so that I am forced to wear the sky

I make the triangle doubt its vertices   the circle doubt its

radius

I make bread suspicious of salt

Will a fixed habit leap out of its orbit?

Am I a fish that hates water?

It is older than stone, this muscle

It has crossed all rationale for stupor

It has discovered oceans of nonsense

With them we followed the arc of a sunflower

We lived with them among the angels' grass

The road is made of limbs and motions

There is no difference between the moon and its shadow

the bird and its branch

And I see the sea through the forest's skirts

Ice becomes king of water   The sun guarded me, the galaxy's

circumference was my orbit

A ram's horn carries me, a bull's lips choose me

I witness how light becomes the body of thorns

how mud releases the moans of the sky

how truth erases me and delusion roots me   How do I cross the distances

between them?

There is always a distance between us

You striking into the artery of distance, surrender
        to the wind that scatters space into bits
        to space that walks with the feet of a child
        to love that has become the exile of love

A Piece of a Secret History of Death →

Goodbye to the body with whom he leapt and that has now walled
        its limbs
Goodbye to a high tide that hides between the childhood of his body
        and the old age of his dreams
Peace to his dying kingdom

A Piece from the Book of Stories

        He erases desire   discovers it
        Thorns are the hands of whoever plants flowers
        The angel is the beginning of the animal

            He erases   discovers
    He dreams with the body he writes
but the words are dreams and the writing is a woman
who had died: Is love love?
He can no longer see—I mean he can see now

When death visits him he will not hear her voice
and if she asked him, Who am I? he will not know the answer
Perhaps he'll whisper, have we truly met?
and say,
                a new name for love now rises

A Piece of Bahlul's Sun

To be what he is
he exited himself—exited
                and someone he does not know   now lives there

I tuck night under my arm
an offering to each body   I convey this message:
                Reach out   the way the sea reaches dry land →
                They attach, but there is no bond between them
                Each is the other's contrary

—But Bahlul, why am I beautiful?
—Because a ship sees you, not a wave

5.
Night nudes his lovers
                becomes a mystic   unites with his smallest parts
                        Tell the sky to change its name
                        Tell the earth to take my shape

My face is a glimpse into the eye of a drying lake
My body tastes like a shroud

This is why
the thunder of labyrinths snatches at me
This is why
the world becomes a window too small for my eyelashes

I know the shell
        the sea's lantern
        thigh of night   the moon's blade
        tongue of carnation   lip of basil
I know the face and the back of the head
        and there is a surface on which I spread, but I don't know its reaches and colors
        The body to whom I gave my body, I didn't see it
        The body that asked me to read it, I wrote another
                        Write me, I read another
This is why
I echo   as a voice without words on a stage without thresholds
This is why
I hear words without a voice:
        The hand of dawn touched you once
           and disappeared

Seasons, adorn yourself with the candles of a history being extinguished
The grass closes it chambers
Spring breaks its first keys

There are some who wound and insert a fly in the wound
>Here I am
>falling from the second horizon of birth
>and another space is torn up before me

Longing etched on the walls of time
>wake your beasts and release them

Babylonian ink
>retrieve your stupor and become drunk on me
>>My time is a shirt tightening and desire is a body expanding
>>I erase you, Desire
>>>I discover you →

In the pool I hear horses neighing
I see the stretch of flatlands in a navel
>a muscle turning
>a muscle that resists me
>a muscle that turns some of me against me

I touch the cranium and the heart
>>the pulse of bones
>>the drone of arteries

Your face spills out as my blood
and I take and I repeat and I mumble
>The horizon is the smoke of hope

Let my body find its balance on paper

A pathway	and your steps are the trees
A scene	and your body is the actor and the play
A shadow	and your body is the waves and gesticulations
A surface	and your body is the depth

Letters   and your body is the writing
And you stroll on
inside a shroud you wove thread by thread
Tell the needles to slow
          and you too slow down

Labyrinths of love
I foresaw you and my eyes beheld you
I cooled you, froze you
I became your swamp, I bridged you
I am now the breeze blowing on you
and my body is a tremor inside you

A Piece of Bahlul's Sun →

He erases desire   discovers it
          he tumbles into it
          her embrace is dispersals and reunions
He reigned her over his body
He accompanied her with his breaths and enthroned her
He mapped her into an elixir and surveyed his illness
They preyed on each other
and one of them ate the other
          He has no words for what is revealed to him

Then

she traps him in a tunnel

a species of a spider web

He fights with a wing that fell off a dead fly

He imagines an eagle followed by the sun who follows a dying star and says

This is how I live

He imagines a canary killed by the hands that soothes it and says

This is how I love

From dream

to dream

he proceeds → hope closes in on its last autumn

and love is like water and grass

no roof except delusion

no delusion except the depths

and the wave said

I am the future

I erase my body   I discover my body →

You said to me: You complain of solitude

You said: I will embody love for you:

a branch

covered with thorns

inserted into the lover's cavern

each thorn clings to a vein

then it's pulled

and it takes what it takes and it leaves what it leaves

My cells multiplied and became larger than the sea

I slide on the slope of an unknown hollow

My language crawls on the edge of an abyss
       and between the ecstasy of sunflowers
          and the lips of an invisible demise
I dangle
                      No   almost
                    between
                 in
              Perhaps   n/ever
and denial is an epoch and each epoch is an object   a flame that drags the body's
    alphabet
       and dies out

My body is made of things contradicting each other
      It ties its shroud to the foot of the sun
and says to a moth
with the color in my face
        "write me on your wings
          and burn" →
This is how
I slide into shapes   masculine and feminine
Memory has a curtain that smothers me
Movement has symbols that erase memory
        They bared my surroundings from below
        They covered my surroundings from above
     My body is a line   My wrinkles are expressions
—Are you kin to what is written?
—Are you kin to what is said?
            It is more eloquent

to wear engravings and codes

more profound

that my limbs become margins and appendices

more transparent

that time becomes a flower wilting (or opening) where my face is its vase

Skin equivocates

I delve into the pathways of the depths

I revolve

I tumble

I break into tidal waves

and my terrors stream →

The wound is Delta

the balsam is Alpha

and the body is an alphabet without its dots

What abyss can fit me now?

The place has no reed for me to lean on   its climate has no clouds to predict

rain

Now in my body I hear

branches being cut

limbs flying off

I stream into shrapnel

then wilt

Love-Mind that the body tears into strips

Love, you who are the essence of water

widen

become ruin and sun
settle dust down with dust

Open into your stages, body, from now to death →
—When were you born and how old are you?
—I do not count, I am not numbered
I collapse and I am distracted
My whims overwhelm my motions and soak my face with despair
I repeat: I own regions that I do not know
Ash turns me into legions, and flames drag me before them →

A Piece of a Secret History of Death →

      Expand, dear fog, expand my blood and strengthen vigilance
There are waves coming from invisible shores
        saying they are what I foresaw
    There is clay that has changed its name
    a letter that has spun away from the sound it makes
a horizon on the lip of the horizon
      saying it is what I foresaw
and between nerve and nerve there is a desert
      saying it is what I foresaw

And you, flower of pain, offer me other possibilities
      become motherhood   a flower with thousands of patterns and hammers
        cups and coronets

Offer me—remember my face
You used to lean close toward it whenever we gathered by water or air to read death
       and our scents mingled
       and our limbs became pairs of twins
I tell you, woman: You will die taken by water
You tell me: You will die taken by the sun

But
in a instant you wilt between my eyes →
       We are separated by flame and flame and flame
           and the labyrinths of Sunday, Saturday, Friday, Thursday
I link desire and the taste of dirt within you
       happiness with the flavor of death
       Here is my body
           tattooed with spots of regret
           crawling between my words
       The jungles of insomnia thicken
       Mountains rise before me
           Trees sleep
           and all the pebbles turn their ears toward me

I imagine that a hand is a hand and a face is a face
I do so in sympathy with the sand

A Piece of Bahlul's Sun

The body remembers	Love forgets
Love is to leave	The body is to arrive
Love is to imagine	The body is to lose one's mind
Love, a cosmic farce	

so that eternity remains distended

so that we soothe our doubt

A Second Piece

Love is the angel of dispossession

a child who remains in its birth labors

Love is clothing   the more lovers there are, the less love

A bed inhabited by divine insects spluttering the ravings of the universe

where the thigh of the moon is entangled with the leg of a mouse

and the sun's jaw and a lizard's tongue embrace

Love is a mouth mispronounced from its home

Don't ask for ecstasy out of love

don't ask of it in contempt

Ask for it as ceaseless mist

from a cloud swimming

in a wandering space that swims

in the space of a desire that has no name

that has no name

A Third Piece

Since the sky began to feed the earth
her sad face split in two:
                        one half for error
                        one for regret

Error is too early
Regret is too late
and man is torn between them

6.

His ghosts said
            you slept with the last star   rose with the first sparrow
            your body behind your body and your eyes shyly hid themselves
            You drew maps of water knowing water escapes and erases
            You asked how a premonition becomes a pair of hands and a pair of feet
            and you said imagination touches my fingers
                        The place imagines me
                        What does an eye need an eye for?

The afternoon shed its skin and became a body
the horizon moss
thorns made of water

And his ghosts said, failure, you are his second body
Only you knew him   You said

there are saplings inside him and machines
to banish what he embraces and to banish what he exempts
And you told all things to wear him
and you told him, dress yourself with me
                    Now you can begin

The body was new and told us:
            My aim is to name fever the body's memory
            my aim to speak with the fires within
            my aim to oppose the waves so that I can misguide the shores
                    and begin falling
                            into
                            the opulence
                            of strength

And the body was new and told us:
            Water is too tight for my thirst
            and I am too narrow for my "I"
            I have a thousand tongues and possess only one word
            I have countless kinds of death
                    and I have only one grave

And his ghosts said: Wet yourself with the rain of things and smother them, grass of
            language
                            He invents his organs, his enemies
                            He reads the history of dust
                            and he crowns matter as the king of his symbols

And you, columns of memory, go ahead and blow yourself up
And you, ember of the past, go ahead and put yourself out
       He empties his body of the names crowded within it
       He offers them to a body that has no name
       and he loves this body that has no name

And his ghosts said: his surroundings devour him
       his pickaxe uproots him
       his hands tear him up
From his ruins walls rose and his palaces stood tall
His shadow split itself in two and both claim to love him
       One adores his corpse
       the other prefers a silence that resembles it
       and his corpse spread as an ether
       from which heads and thighs dangle   tables
                       and beds

         and his corpse spread as a mirror
         spread along the ruins of the horizon
         And everything began to reflect itself in it:
Where is the sparrow?   It flies with wings of mud
Where is the cockroach?   It wears the face of an angel

And his ghosts said: misery, melt him and drip him as the rain of time
       His organs have grown bored with their names
       with pronunciation and silence
       with stasis and movement

His organs have grown bored with him   they pass him—he follows them
Melt him, misery, so that he knows if he is he, or someone else

And his ghosts said: Let's move on
          Before us the body is piling itself upon itself
                              secret by secret
          Rot is also a heart
          rot is also childhood
          rot is also what love is

so that we are convinced
          that love is   to doubt love
          that life is   when your eye beautifies the mud that you are . . .

to become filth and filth becomes what your feasts and festivals will be . . .

And so that we are convinced:
          that life pretends death
that you become from the beginning   dead-alive
                    alive-dead

And his ghosts said: in the name of your body, dead-alive, alive-dead body
                    you are not on the edge
                    you are not in the middle
                    you are not wise
                    you are not wild
                    you are
          fall   and rise

the moment you breathe and that repeats

        a word   not a word

        something   nothing

    Absent what is before   Absent yourself

and enter the festivals of erasure and thunder   aim   release

        a command is not a command

        a forbiddance is not a forbiddance

    Pull out your blood thread by thread

        follow it

        become violent   turn to kindness

    penetrate →

        without direction

        without method

        collisions

        leaps

        do not try to overtake others

    burn   thrive

    become the place that has no place

        time that defeats time

    become desire desire desire

        conjure the body

        name it your messenger

        your mouthpiece

7.

In the name of my dead-alive body   alive-dead

        body has no shape

        my body has as many shapes as its pores

and I am not I
and you, woman, are not you
    and we correct our pronunciation and our tongues
    and we invent words the size of tongues and lips
        and chin
        and the beginning of throat
    and our bodies enter the depths of jungles and weddings
        They collapse
        they build themselves
        in the gales
        of feasting
        that has no shape →
           slow   fast
           toward what we named life
           and was the beginning of death

In the name of my dead-alive body, alive-dead
    cedars rise between my name and face
    language returns to her first house
    Love was a grave I entered and abandoned
    and the grave a stroll I took to give my arteries some rest
Grammar and conjugation died
They were stuffed into the hands of my first poem and my last
and this throng of words began to rule and arbitrate
    vindicate   and indict
    so that night arrives
    so that daylight flees the day

and daylight comes
        to chase night out of night
and so that the earth keeps the memory of grass
        it covers itself with straw

In the name of my dead-alive body, alive-dead
        now the body can distinguish between my body and itself
He can capture one organ with another
        fight one cell with another
He can plant my blood and harvest it
        and my body can be my body
        → against my body

8.

INVOCATIONS

A:

Peace to you body
        music   released by pleasure as melodies that guided me
                I loved them and delighted in them
I arranged the four chords according to the four types:

singular   yellow bile
dual   blood
tripartite   phlegm
quartet   black bile

and I ran the rhythm through countless rivers
        Peace to you, body

B:

Come near me, olive tree

     let this refugee embrace you

          and sleep in your shade

               Let him pour his life on your good trunk and allow him to call you:

                    woman

C:

"At night

we, the women, leave our beds

we go naked to the edges of the village

we carry wands the color of dirt

we spray water on them

we lie on the dark earth

        then there is cloud

        then there is rain"

D:

Lie down, beautiful woman

        on this beautiful grass

        place a beautiful flower between your thighs

        and tell your beautiful lover

            to remove it with his most beautiful part

E:

Strip naked, rose tree, wear the moon

Come down, master Moon   wrap yourself in the rose tree

        We have placed a ladder for you

We made the rose tree's foot the last of the ladder's steps
adorned it with other flowers
decorated it with etchings and drawings
of roosters in the wild
of eels in the sea
so that we see the wedding of sky and earth

F:

You, who were followed by a woman
who covered herself with scraps of schoolbooks
and wrapped her head with rose coronets
her name was Princess of the Grasses
and her name was Feast Day
and her name was Words
You who have gone
we are now besieging your name
circling it
believing you are a tree
We break you branch by branch
make a doll out of you, wrap it with straw
and toss it to the foam

And we say:

foam
too
is one
of the
sea's
keys

G:
Bring me a strand of your hair
    tie it to a branch
      place it in an embrace as wide as the wind's horizon
      in the eyes of lovers

9.
Peace to corruption peaceable as air
natural as if it were genesis itself
Peace to unseen machines I invent to create my other bodies
            other hearts
Peace to my star sitting on the edge of the chain
      who makes borders out of my foot and arms and flags
Peace to my face   following a moth following fire

Shall I separate myself from myself?
Shall I mate with it   Is mat
ing a moment of singularity or doubl
ing? Shall I take up another face? and wh
at does a body do that is spotted with wounds that do not he
al? It is the desert
      closing in on me   locusts
gnawing at my peripheries

Death, sit somewhere else
and let's swap faces
      I make out of my pulse a sap for my alphabet

I make you skin
I name you vision
          the taste of things
          and declare
I am the idolater and destruction is my worship

And man, I say in your name:
          smile, river, to your drought
          rejoice, flower, between thorn and thorn

And I say in your name:
          in ashen things I open a body and scan its realms
          where the rainbow walks with the steps of a child
          and my imagination can prey on my eye
                    and destroy the bridges between me and what is around me
          and I may rise and catch the surrounding air

And man, I say in your name, whispering to your ghosts:
                    perfumes that exude desire
                    adorn yourselves
                    and become my air

And I say in your name:
          always on the lip of madness
          but I never go mad

Sit down, dear death, in another place and let's swap faces

    I name you "body" and ask →

        how can I live with   the body I accuse

        when I am the accused, witness, and judge?

And I name you my body

        and I look to you   to it   breaking apart and assembling

        the arm   a leg

        the wrist   an ankle

        the hand   a foot

        the shoulder   an elbow

        and what remains is not what remains

        and I surrender, I the steadfast one

        like an avalanche

        my neck falls into the clavicle

        which falls into my chest

        and the chest falls into the backside

           and the buttocks fall into the thighs

  and the thighs become lead sinking at my feet

        and my muscles light

           up with their own light

And she says in my name

    I name you lover

        a face for the animal

        a face for the vegetable

    I listen to your hallucinations rising

        among the panting of the elements:

Dhal ذ Ta ت:
—Woman, my state follows your motions
Night and day are my letters to you
            They urge each other like two mares in a race
How can I quell my upheavals
while the need for you has beaten me?

Wawu و Nuun ن:
How do I quell my upheavals
when need for you has beaten me?
            Are you weeping?
Fire will not burn a place touched by tears
            This is why I weep
Carnation grows in tears
            This is why I weep
Yesterday I read: "Each desire is cruelty except
                        mating → it softens and purifies"
            This is why I weep

Siin س   Alif ا:
—Enter, woman, as if you have made a hole through hell and left it or
            like a woman buying perfume with bread
                  I count you and find some of you missing
                  I become time within you, I planet my parts around you
I had befriended myself in you
            and when I followed you

I said

>   parts of the self
>   chase after one another

But
why am I too much for myself and too little with you
why, whenever you come near me, I feel as if a part of me has disappeared
>   Nonetheless, enter
>   My body is still moist with your memory
But how can I quell my upheavals
when need for you has beaten me?

And in your name, man,   I say to her body
>   your body is my voice   I hear it
>   my vision lay scattered in it   your body is my departure and each cell
is a leaping point
Your body is my harbor   I mislead the ports   Your body is stone
and aims to keep me
>   Dust flies me
>   Your body is my oblivion
>   and it shades me
>   Your body is your realm and I am its winged beasts
>   your body a rainbow and I am climate and change

And man, I ask in your name
Have I become desert   no shelter in me
Have I befriended someone who purifies me?
>   Whoever shields me from words

falls to grief
and from signs
shrinks to nothing
How will the cage be broken open then?

And she says in my name,
invent for your body what contradicts it
become a gust of wind and pebbles in one body
complete your body with its negation
let language take the shape of the body
let poetry be its rhythm

Sit, dear death, in another place and let's swap faces
I say in my name and yours
we misguide life and it steers us on
What shall I do
when my body is wider than the space that contains it
when I am the seeker
and there is nothing but death before me?

And we say in her name, in your name, in my name
Because of you I have crystallized
and now wish to be obliterated
I opened you with my body → but
how do I seal you?
And though I am corrupted with you
I am a thing that leans on no-thing

not tied
or welded
not opening—
I flow   without stopping
and my body tumbles with it, and falls
            between two parentheses about to re-unify
I am the healthy-ill   the meridian of sex →
            I conquered
            defeated the "how much" and the "how"
            crossed past all that is said

Still,
I have grown tired of your image on regions and layers . . .
        I seek divine protection for our names from all certainty
        (certainty is the trap of conscience
                and to know
                is to
                know → and not know)

This is how I move in the chains of my madness and I vary the links
this one, my steadfast one
        my changeling
        my rock-like
        body
and this way
        and this way
        and this

This is how I ask:

     you are my path, how do I walk you?

          or

          ask

     Are you a false legend told about me?

This way

          I deny all that breaks me apart

          and all that gathers me

And man, I say in your name:

          I am water playing with water

The Book of Similarities and Beginnings

1980

SEARCH

/ . . . A bird
spreading its wings—   Is it afraid
     the sky will fall?   Or that the
     wind is a book inside its feathers?
                           The neck

     latches to the horizon
     and the wings are words
     swimming in a labyrinth . . . /

THE POETS

No place for them,   —they warm
     the earth's body,   they make
     for space   its keys   —
       They do not create
       a lineage   or a home
       for their myths,   —
They write them
the way the sun writes its history,   —
No place . . .

THE EXPERIMENT

Fine, I will not sleep
I'll study these roads, and know what the others know.
Fine, I'll join this crowd, —
        a step, two steps, three . . . /
                a dead man, a policeman
                a dead man, a policeman
                a dead man, a policeman . . . /
/ And you will not be a witness against us /

Here I am in the ocean of words
sheets floating on top, —   and I see that I am repeating what others have said
and I see that I am asleep.

CHILDREN

Children read the book of the present, and say,
       this is a time that blossoms
       in the wombs of torn limbs.
They write,
this is a time where we see
how death rears the earth,
and how water betrays water.

PRODIGAL

No horizon between us—
      the trees of love were dust
      and night was a carriage ferrying my steps   ferrying the desert toward itself.
No horizon between us—
      the hour was nakedness
      and my death was cloth:
Inheritor of sand
carrying black stones for bread,
the sun is his water and his shade.

THE BEGINNING OF DOUBT

Here I am being born—
seeking people.
      I love this sighing, this space.
      I love this dust that covers brows. I am illuminated.
I seek people—a spring and sparks.
I read my drawings, nothing but longing,
            and this glory
in people's dust.

THE BEGINNING OF POETRY

The best thing one can be is a horizon.
     And the others?   Some will think you are the call
          others will think you are its echo.
The best thing one can be is an alibi
     for light and darkness
where the last words are your first.
And the others?   Some will see you as the foam of creation
          others will think you the creator.
The best thing one can be is a target—
       a crossroad
       between silence and words.

THE BEGINNING OF THE BOOK

A subject or a pronoun—
        and time is the adjective.   What?   Did you speak,
              or is something
              speaking in your name?

What to borrow? Metaphor is a cover
        and a cover is loss—
        Here is your life being invaded by words.
        Dictionaries do not give away their secrets.   Words
              do not answer, they go on questioning—   loss
        and metaphor   a transition
        from one fire to another
        one death to another.

You are this passage being deciphered,
              born in each interpretation:
There will be no way
to describe your face.

THE BEGINNING OF LOVE

Lovers read their wounds, and we wrote them
      as another era, then drew
      our time:
      My face is evening, your eyelashes are dawn.
Our steps are blood and longing
      like theirs.

Every time they awoke, they plucked us
and tossed their love away and tossed us—
a flower in the wind.

THE BEGINNING OF THE ROAD

Night was paper and we were
      ink:

—"Did you draw a face, or a stone?"
—"Did you draw a face, or a stone?"
      I did not answer
      nor did she. Our love

our silence—has no inroads
like our love—no road leads to it.

THE BEGINNING OF SEX

Rooms bend inside our arms, sex raises its towers—
A fall, a tumble
into a bay of sadness
a sadness
in the bays of our waists—sex opens its doors—and we enter.
Fire was sowing, night is harvesting its candles—We make a cradle out
of a hill, we fill the crater in, we whisper
to the horizon to give us its hands.
The light of bitterness is like a river whose banks
have gotten lost. We make its water
ours, and turn our banks
into a cloth
to cover love's shores.

THE BEGINNING OF THE NAME

My days are her name
and the dream, when the sky spends its night inside my sadness, is her name.
Premonition is her name
and the feast, when the slaughterer and the slaughtered are one, is her name.

Once I sang: every rose
in fatigue is her name
in travel, her name.

Has the road come to an end? Has she changed her name?

THE BEGINNING OF ENCOUNTER

A man and a woman,
reeds entangle them, reeds and moans.
Rain and dust meet,—
          heaps of rubble collapse,
          and from the language of ash, a spark.

Where is the oncoming cloud,
where is the book of sorrow? I ask—
          Your eyes are bewilderment
          and your face hears no questions.

I am the end of night
I love so that I begin.

And I say, they met
          a man and a woman
          a man and a woman . . .

THE BEGINNING OF SEX II

A room   balconies   darkness

the remains of wounds
a body breaking apart—
sleep

between one loss and another

Our bloods spin their dialogue
and our labyrinths are words

THE BEGINNING OF WIND

"The body of the night"
                    she said
                    "is a house
          of wounds and their days . . . "

We begin the way dawn begins.   We enter shade and our dreams entangle.
The sun opens her flowers: "Foam
will come dressed up as the sea"—

                    We try to measure
our distances.   We rise
and see to the winds that erase our traces.

                    We whisper
to recall our times
then we part.

THE BEGINNING OF DEATH

Death rises in steps—his shoulders:
                a woman and a swan.

Death descends in steps—his feet:
                sparks and the remains
               of extinguished cities.

And the sky that was all wings, expands
          and expands—

THE BEGINNING OF PRONUNCIATION

We can now ask about how we met
we can now utter the road of our return
      and say: the beaches are abandoned
           and the forts
tell the story of destruction.

We can now bow and say: We are done for.

THE BEGINNING OF NARRATION

Lead was whizzing past
children were shrapnel or flags.

        —Here are the bodies of the burned
        the slaughtered
        the ones who died for freedom.

Sun spots
and words now, all words
have become Arab.

THE BEGINNING OF SPEECH

That child I was came to me
once,
a strange face.
          He said nothing—   We walked,
each of us glancing at the other in silence, our steps
a strange river running in between

We were brought together by good manners
and these sheets now flying in the wind
then we split,
a forest written by the earth
watered by the seasons' change.

Child who once was, come forth—
What brings us together now,
and what do we have to say?

The Book of Siege

1985

DESERT

The cities dissolve, and the earth is a cart loaded with dust.
Only poetry knows how to pair itself to this space.

No road to his house, a siege,
and his house is graveyard.
>   From a distance, above his house
>   a perplexed moon dangles
>   from threads of dust.

I said: this is the way home, he said: No
>   you can't pass, and aimed his bullet at me.
Very well then, friends and their homes
>   in all of Beirut are my companions.

Road for blood now—
>   Blood about which a boy talked
>   whispered to his friends:
>   nothing remains in the sky now
>   except holes called "stars."

The city's voice was too tender, even the winds
would not tune its strings—
The city's face beamed

like a child arranging his dreams for nightfall
bidding the morning to sit beside him on his chair.

They found people in bags:
      a person   without a head
      a person   without hands, or tongue
      a person   choked to death
      and the rest had no shapes and no names.
            —Are you mad? Please
                        don't write about these things.
A page in a book
      bombs mirror themselves inside of it
      prophecies and dust-proverbs mirror themselves inside of it
      cloisters mirror themselves inside of it, a carpet made of the alphabet
            disentangles thread by thread
falls on the face of the city, slipping out of the needles of memory.
A murderer in the city's air, swimming through its wound—
its wound is a fall
that trembled to its name—to the hemorrhage of its name
and all that surrounds us—
Houses left their walls behind
            and I am no longer I.

Maybe there will come a time in which you'll accept
to live deaf and mute, maybe
they'll allow you to mumble: death
            and life

> resurrection
> and peace unto you.

From the wine of the palms to the quiet of the desert . . . et cetera
from a morning that smuggles its own intestines
> and sleeps on the corpses of the rebels . . . et cetera
from streets, to trucks
> from soldiers, armies . . . et cetera
from the shadows of men and women . . . et cetera
from bombs hidden in the prayers of monotheists and infidels . . . et cetera
from iron that oozes iron and bleeds flesh . . . et cetera
from fields that long for wheat, and grass and working hands . . . et cetera
from forts that wall our bodies
> and heap darkness upon us . . . et cetera
from legends of the dead who pronounce life, who steer our life . . . et cetera
from talk that is slaughter   and slaughter   and slitters of throats . . . et cetera
from darkness to darkness to darkness
I breathe, touch my body, search for myself
> and for you, and for him, and for the others

and I hang my death
between my face and this hemorrhage of talk . . . et cetera

You will see—
> say his name
> say you drew his face
> reach out your hand toward him

or smile
or say I was happy once
or say I was sad once
you will see:
                    there is no country there.

Murder has changed the city's shape—this stone
                                is a child's head—
and this smoke is exhaled from human lungs.
Each thing recites its exile . . .   a sea
                    of blood—and what
do you expect on these mornings except their arteries set to sail
into the darkness, into the tidal wave of slaughter?

Stay up with her, don't let up—
she sits death in her embrace
and turns over her days
                    tattered sheets of paper.
Guard the last pictures
of her topography—
she is tossing and turning in the sand
in an ocean of sparks—
on her bodies
are spots of human moans.

Seed after seed are cast into our earth—
fields feeding on our legends,
guard the secret of these bloods.

> I am talking about a flavor to the seasons
> and a flash of lightning in the sky.

Tower Square—(an engraving whispers its secrets
> to bombed-out bridges . . .)
Tower Square—(a memory seeks its shape
> among dust and fire . . .)
Tower Square—(an open desert
> chosen by winds and vomited . . . by them . . .)
Tower Square—(It's magical
> to see corpses move/their limbs
> in one alleyway, and their ghosts
> in another/and to hear their sighs . . .)
Tower Square—(West and East
> and gallows are set up—
> martyrs, commands . . .)
Tower Square—(a throng
> of caravans: myrrh
> and gum Arabica and musk
> and spices that launch the festival . . .)
Tower Square—(let go of time . . .
> in the name of place)

—Corpses or destruction,
        is this the face of Beirut?
—and this
        a bell, or a scream?
—A friend?
—You? Welcome.
        Did you travel? Have you returned? What's new with you?
—A neighbor got killed . . . /

. . . .

A game/
—Your dice are on a streak.
—Oh, just a coincidence /

        . . . .

        Layers of darkness
        and talk dragging more talk.

PERSONS

Ahmad . . .
stars under his eyelashes
and spiders weave his dreams.

Suleiman shines with his own centrifugal pull—
he says, I found my way, then lets go of his eyelids
            to the light that shined inside his house.
The face of the world outside was a crow on his windowsill.

Qassim did not say, "the dream carries an axe."
"The dream heads to its field," is what he said.

An oleander burst out crying
when Ali covered his face with its petals—
He was weeping for the birds that left
paying his condolences to the sky.

Suddenly, at the intersection of two paths,   a face—
            Is it him? But he died, or it was said he died. Noise
                        cars
            sellers of lettuce and tobacco.

Should I call him? I call—a face—
            I could not distinguish its features, he answered . . . Hello
What is his name?
            Noise and bullets—suddenly a droning
the sound of a truck . . .

Every day
he awakes before the sun, to see out from the balcony
                                    how flowers
greet dawn's first steps.

—How does space enter his bloody room?
—The high fires of his limbs.

Apologize
to the paths that your steps have led
astray and succumb
            to the prophetic darkness—
you are more than a trespasser into this Arab ascent.

Neither these orbits nor this hurtling language
could tempt you out of the city's wounds.
            It was you who surrendered to a passing moment—
your steps

are nothing but prey being chased in the wilds of memory.
Your body is now a candle of doubt
and the place is a torrent of terror. Your eyes do not close
afraid the place will abandon them.

I don't want you to talk or gesture. It's better
       that you remain an absence
       so that you remain a question.

This was an alleyway to her house—many times
the trees there hid us—and on its features
we drew our steps.
Here Marwan brought his friends together
and their covenant died along with them
and erased these steps with it.
They took him to a hole, burned him.
       He was not a murderer, he was a child.
       He was not . . .   was a voice
rose like a wave, rose with the fire, rose in steps of space
and he is now a reed flute suspended in the air.

Her kerchief was not to mask his face
       or to block the dust or wipe away tears, her kerchief
       was a plate of bread, cheese and eggs, and it was a wrapping
for her machine gun
and her kerchief was a flag.

He left the caravan
          its trumpets and raucous air—
alone and wilted—
and that wilting flower
pulled him toward her scent.

You'll continue to be my friend
between what was, and what remains
among all this ruin.
You'll be my friend, light
that dresses itself in cloud, O master that never sleeps.

He did not notice clouds, did not notice fire.
From where will the water come?
Will he drag his steps toward words
and follow the caravan of things?

She took a piece of bread /   the child
was playing with her cane
and pitter-pattered in her footsteps.
                    She carried him like a jewel, flooded him
                    smothered him with her face
                    and went on limping   her cane
                    an inheritance from a father
                    who was murdered.

Day is a loaf of bread
and evening is its duration . . .
and evening is a loaf of bread
and day is its duration—
                    paper blowing in its wind.
Winter will be long—
spring will die without song—

Is this an elegy for Laila who had not died?

Whether you were someone or no one
a flash of lightning or a cloud of ash
among the severed limbs of this age   whether you were tossed into the darkness
            of the abyss
or covered with mountains of foam
you are still the flavor of dawn, you are the light of distances,
                            you this horizon of
        your suns, you this echo that still resonates.
For your song—my voice chokes up, my storms hesitate
and when I sing you at last, your face remains your face,
            but your death becomes mine
except that I am alive inside a hemorrhage of your wound
                            and within the fire of its pain I explode.
            I clear a space in myself   for myself . . .
Your blood sepulcher reconciles me with my life.
Like you I travel deep into tragedy, massacre and terror

dig into your steps and mine,
and death becomes our Arab predator.

You died, but you are now my song and my companion.
I am not of you, but I belong to your murmuring, to whatever storms and torrents blow
      between your arms
and your path is not my way to light, but it is my path
and I am now closer to you than yourself.
And when I approach your death, I ask, "Are my feet on the ground?
                  Is my body firm and set?"
Do you think I am hung in a space of terror surrendered
                            and dangling?
And when I lean toward your death I ask, "Are you closer to me than I?"
and I ask,
         "is earth my country
         or is my country the death of your alphabet?"

Let's say, there was a covenant of sap between us
         a road from root to blossom.
Let's say, whatever there was between the first clot and its creator is now broken
let's say, we begin now in the migration of the wind through the forest of sparks
and let's walk, not to this place, or to that place.
Let's walk to where there is nothing but road and this vow between us—
We are a fire of pull and push, our visions
and steps are an orbit
for the myth of our time.

CANDLELIGHT

Through the years of the civil war, especially during the siege, I learned to create an intimate relationship with darkness, and I began to live in another light that does not come from electricity, or butane, or kerosene.

I despise these last two lamps,
they spew a foul odor that kills the sense of smell and poisons the childhood of the air and the air of childhood. They repel the eyes with a beam that pierces vision like a needle.

Moreover they bring petroleum to mind and how it has transformed Arab life into a dark state of confusion and loss.

The other light I love is the light of a candle.

An impulse makes me wonder, was this new companionship a celebration of childhood or a desire to celebrate it? Was it a way to tap into the imagination of our ancestors hoping for more than the poetry they left behind? Perhaps I longed to attach myself to the body of the alphabet, as it had been imagined by that wrongheaded Phoenician who invented it and suffered the consequences of his invention. I say wrongheaded, and I ask him across the distances that separate us and unite us, why did you not let us write with the bodies of things, the things themselves, and not these letters steeped in abstraction? Isn't matter closer to man's nature, more deserving and expressive than these signs and symbols? And can you prove, that you and your offspring who improvised upon your invention in this city of Beirut, that the writer who inscribes letters and words and writes in bundles is more reasonable and understanding than another who only sings words and runs them between his lips? You yourself can see that those who took up your invention made a swamp of the world with noises that pollute everything, while the other transformed sounds into musical chords where the voices rising from the throats of nature intermingle and soar.

I chose candlelight as my companion though I never cared for the shape or color of the thing itself. The one I have here is sky blue, an unusual find, and I had no choice in the matter. That was determined by what was made available to me, and that in turn was determined by time and circumstance.

A skyblue candle . . . It set me in a mood reminiscent of lives spent in caves, caves that led to our first conscious choice, which ties us to the first womb of our knowing: our exodus from the world's night to its day, from the dimness Plato spoke of to bright life, from delusion to truth.

But have we truly left the world's darkness? I wondered as I watched the shadow the candle spread on the ground or on the wall, and the shadow my own head made. And I began to realize to my own dismay that this shadow we call delusion is not less real than myself or the candle. And I said, as I witnessed death snatch many around me with the speed of a wink, that we still stand with our backs to the sun. Perhaps Plato was the first to make this mistake and we have persisted since then in separating shadow from light, truth from illusion, setting eternal boundaries between them. But where does illusion begin and truth end?

A candle in a skyblue dress . . .
Some of us perceived "light" and "truth" according to Plato as only an ascent on the ladder of electricity, and the higher one rises, the more deserving he becomes of plucking a star and making a throne for himself out of it. This may explain the reason why people looked at candlelight with a degree of revulsion and contempt . . .

I was among a few who were taken instead by the notion of descent, by shade, this transparent night that braces vagueness and clarity, making them move as a single wave. We used to say that illusion, or what was called illusion, was nothing but a truth our visions have yet to discern, and what was called truth was nothing but an illusion we have exhausted. We used to say that the normal state of things is shadow, and light is its transitory condition. For if the whole world had turned into light, or to an electric light, the whole world would lose its secrets, beauty, and attractiveness. So I sided with shadow and shade, and accordingly, I sided with the candlelight while others sided with bright electric light. Their enthusiasm grew from their belief that electricity was the offspring of an ancient Phoenician energy that had existed for only a short while, only to appear again in a non-Phoenician shape somewhere else.

This energy was symbolically, or let's say mythologically, represented, in a Lebanese, Greek, Syrian woman whose name was Electra. She, of course, was Cadmus's sister and he, a Phoenician who brought the alphabet to the West, Greece to be precise. She was the daughter of Atlas who carried the sky on his shoulders, and niece of Prometheus who stole fire from the gods and gave it to mankind. From Cadmus's line comes Euclid, who was the first teacher of optics (or let's say electricity) in the Egyptian temples, focusing mainly on yellow amber out of which the most beautiful prayer beads are made.

I wish to remind those who do not like prayer beads but love electricity of something they do not know, or ignore: only through touching prayer beads can we touch electricity. This amber body that rubs against ours without shocking us due to the quality of its shadowy light is a transparent night dressed in stone. How pleasurable it would be, dear reader, for you to hear my friend Samir Sayyigh talk about this electrified body of amber and the electricity embodied in it. When Samir speaks of prayer beads, examining them and running them over the tips of his fingers, or gently touching them with his lips, you begin to feel as if a great many clouds are gathering, and that lightning is about to strike and overwhelm the place.

And Euclid himself is an early example of the interaction between the Phoenician/Egyptian and Greek sensibilities. I have read also that Euclid was as long ago as 610 B.C. the first to predict a solar eclipse.

I was recalling this mythological history as I sat in candlelight and compared it with the living history we were experiencing then minute by minute, written with iron and fire, rockets and bombs, and with human limbs, by our cousins, ancestors of Moses and Solomon who are among our own prophets. Solomon, tradition says, had a way of speaking with inanimate objects and living things. And Moses was the first human to whom God had spoken, a singular honor indeed.

I was comparing this mythological, pagan history and this real Godcentric history that we live today, and so I wish to register my surprise:

There was man who never spoke to God or never even knew of him, and who had no light except candlelight. He nonetheless was able to create a history that lifts mankind and the whole world and that opened before them horizons where they could proceed endlessly.

And here was man to whom God had spoken and whom he preferred over the whole of creation, granting him electricity as if it were a dromedary crouching at his feet, and he creates his history beginning with murder then descending endlessly into an abyss of severed limbs and blood.

As I was thinking and deducing, I embraced the slim shadow of the candle and began to whisper some of my secrets to it. Then I turned toward the Mediterranean and listened to its groaning not far from our bodies, half frozen from confusion and terror, or from death that could strike us at any moment. I turned toward the sea, who invented the light of the world, and began to share in his rocky moaning rising from the ocean's dark.

It's the siege: A flood, but where is the ship, and where shall we go? Nothing awaits us except that mechanical specter, the F-16, that plans to turn us into a golden ash from which a murderous lot among our cousins, the offspring of Moses and Solomon, intends to use for their new crowns and thrones.

Each time the darkness pushed us into it, the candlelight held us, and returned us to its shade and to the real living moment. This is how we rose back to ourselves and their besieged light.

After this departure and return some of us would open a book to evoke another time or mood more than to read per se, especially since some of us have developed elaborate criticisms of reading: How can you read when you are sitting inside the book you read, and as you find yourself moving within each line of it? How can you read when you are what is written and what is read?

As for me, I sought companionship in other things. I imagined that the candle before me has been traveling a road that it has followed from an inherited instinct. A road taken by an ancient grandmother, followed by granddaughters and their granddaughters. I imagined the corners that this candle had inhabited and the people who loved it as it burned between their hands. And often I imagined hearing Abu Nawwas[1] comparing its light with the light of the wine he drank (wine is another electric body and the difference between it and amber is that the first is liquid and the second is solid). And often I imagined the poet Abu Tammam[2] turning in his bed in the light of a dim candle, his eyes have reddened and he in vain is trying to sleep and failing because his limbs are on fire. I also imagined that this candlelight would not attract poetry's other clowns and brigands who, in this human desert, would have preferred the light of the stars. Sometimes I imagined the Sufis and I could almost touch their longing to melt in God the way a candle melted before their eyes.

Candlelight does not lift the covers over the one who is lost alone in the past or the present; it lifts the covers off the faces that remain beside you as you sit or lie awake late into the night, witnessing their bodies melting drop by drop.

The faces of the people who lived in our building would throng and gather around the light of a candle, creating a panorama of wrinkles, features, countenances, blank gazes and quizzical looks:

a face of a still lake without the flutter of a single sail

a face in the shade like that of a sheep led to the slaughterhouse

a face drowned in its sorrows like a hole in the darkness

a face, a white page open to the silence

a face, a sieve through which words drop and spread in all directions

a face, a book in which you can only read forgetfulness, or more correctly, the desire to
       forget

a face of a woman who is a man

a face of a man who is a woman.

The light lifted the cover that concealed the candle from which it shined, and the candle who is the mistress of silence, and who burned without moaning or seeking help, is another face of night even though superficially it belongs to the day. Candlelight illuminates but it does not spread the day. It makes night denser and more present. Candlelight allows revelation, but does not reveal itself.

The candle is the light in liquid shape, is a night inside night, or night weeping, or night wiping its eyes with the edge of a distant star, or night dressed in a nightgown, or night when its desires have awoken . . .

A candle has a bed, but lacks a pillow and does not sleep . . . perhaps to dive deeper into the waves of night; perhaps to attach itself into the gorge of another night which is death; perhaps to deepen the meditation of the outside world that blazes—the houses that rove the ether, the bodies pierced by flack, the climates filled with the pollen dust of flesh and bones where bodies that do not know each other embrace and acclimate, the thunderous voices that weave a fabric for a horizon made of ash and embers; perhaps so that we understand that hemispheric dust that carries principles and ethics, virtues and ideals, and their seas, making out of them this expendable dirt that we call the glory of wars and their victories, or so that we become convinced that what was called man was in truth an animal who by mistake became able to walk on two legs.

Once again the candlelight takes us far only so that we return.
Return to the light of the interior at hand, that room at the bottom of the building, which we have called shelter. This is when night takes on the shape of a desired body, a man for a woman, and woman for a man.

This way all time becomes part of night, and in living with it, we begin to see desire dripping from its extremities, and we see how its legs open and close in a motion made more agile and expansive by the small, narrow shelter. We begin to feel that the moon and its sisters, the stars, are an invisible river that sleeps within. Lighthouses from another strange ecology begin to illuminate and reveal to us connections among contradictory things, uniting people who would never meet anywhere else and for any reason.

It would have been easy, in the state we were in, to believe what was said about the ancients, who were called saints in the language of old, how at night light used to drip from the extremities of these blessed beings. Their heads brightened all that surrounded them and they served as guides for the lost.

Taking advantage of the situation he found us in, someone in our group would begin to speak of the virtues that fueled this internal light. He said these saints were inextinguishable, that they were a light that illuminated light as they have dedicated themselves to the shattering of darkness. Our companion compared this light with the loose light spewed by rockets and bombs, affirming that those who spread such a powerful light, though they speak of nothing except freedom and progress, are disseminating nothing but another name for darkness that has no place in nature, a darkness-light intended to put out all light, whatever it may be, and wherever it is found.

And he would continue, assured by the silence of the others and the appreciation some of us have shown, saying that the ancient Egyptian farmer who used to write his dreams and delusions on papyrus paper in the light of a slim candle, or the Phoenician sailor who befriended the waves and shores, was richer and deeper in his humanity and in his perceptions than today's human being who is proud that he rides mechanical specters that can destroy in seconds whole cities, and whole populations with their villages and huts.

The slim candle is about to go out. Good for it. It's as if it too hates that light flashing from rockets and shells, that oppresses the throat of our Mediterranean, tearing at its vocal cords which once sang with distinction in the chorus of humanity's glory.

And you, are you growing bored, dear reader, from this ancient one striking into the depth of history? But don't you too see how poetry can spring out of what we imagine to be poetry's contrary? And don't you also see that what we call reality is nothing but skin that crumbles as soon as you touch it and begins to reveal what hides under it: that other buried reality where the human being is the poetry of the universe.

I said "the universe" not so that I could escape this dark, narrow shelter, but so that I better roam all the expanses it contains, and all the internal light with which it abounds.

A reckless perfume descends the dark stairway to the shelter. Leave the door open, or we'll all choke to death!

The candlelight is not, as it appears to me in this shelter, a light, but another sort of darkness that makes limbs glow with their desire to possess themselves, the desire to know ourselves and to know nothing but ourselves for a brief time, and to be possessed, or in possession, of them. This darkness, this secret light, can wrench you even from your shadow and can toss you into a focal point of luminous explosion. And you begin to feel, you who are unified and coherent, peerless and singular, you feel that you are always in a state of waiting, expecting some event, not on the outside, but inside you, in your guts. It is a condition that could be called cloudiness. You do not know if you are in rain or in sunshine. And darkness no longer becomes darkness, but a climb toward the threshold of an internal light that is just about to glow. This is when it becomes possible to speak of the light of darkness as it would be possible to speak of the darkness of light.

This is how the candle brought me back to the night of meaning—to a deliquescence into the obscurity of existence. The night of meaning— I see, behind its terraces, our first house—the first childhood, and I catch a glimpse of the lantern that I used to seek and in whose light I surrendered to the whims of my body. There I retrieve some of my old habits, how when I slept I placed nothing between the dirt floor and my body except a wool rug—a beautiful bed made of light's dust and the ether of dreams. Sometimes, I was glad to have a rug made of tender reeds.

This is how the electricity of life grew inside my limbs:
Electra was sometimes kind to me then and spent a few hours with me.
And my friends, the poets, used to sit with me and speak of other energies that these suspended modern tubes were incapable of containing.

The night of meaning— I used to feel my body extend inside a stream of sparks. I will try now to translate to my body what remains of that memory:

A. I used to sleep alone,
    afraid that solitude might leave me.

B. It is not possible to make the world more beautiful.
    This is when it comes to an end.

C. Nothing needs me
    because I need everything.

D. Death is near
    because it is an idea not a body
    and love is distant
    because it is a body not an idea.

E. A mountain roofed with fog:
    an adventurous man.
    A forest roofed with fog:
    a woman dreaming.

F. Dreaming is a shore
    for a ship that never docks.
    Nonetheless, I still belong to dreaming.

G. Cleanse your memory
    of every moment that did not know how to meet you.

H. This tree did not return my greeting.
   Is it because I greeted the wind first?

I. My sadness wears night for its dress.
   It has nothing to wear during the day.

J. The road is a sign of happiness
   because it is an eternal crossing.

K. Water is an eternal lover
   for one reason:
   It knows nothing about failure.

L. Death is both a god and a devil.
   This is why no one loves him.

This is another mood that will overtake you in the light of a candle: You seem to yourself to be in your normal conscious state, but it is the body that thinks now, not the soul, rather this tangle of motions we call the body. You'll discover here that what we call thinking has limits, and that it too possesses a body. And we discover that what we call madness is perhaps nothing but the exhilaration of life: a euphoria of body-soul. It's futile then to subjugate the apprehensions and achievements of this being, or to imprison it in any cold, ethical designation. The energy for meditation and the energy for action become one—a motion open to the world, in a world where things are open to the senses, and the senses open to our inner visions, and where our thoughts of reality, mankind, and history crumble into dust.

You cannot stop yourself once you have been illuminated by the light of a candle, you cannot overcome the feeling that you are not in a shelter, but in a ship that is lost and clings to and embraces the high waves of the sea. You begin to confuse things. You come from nowhere and go to nowhere. The West in your step is merely a shadow, and the East is mere soil. And you look at people in this dark extremity and they become things, not made by the hands of God, but by other hands and with another clay: This one is a pistol, and that one a bullet; this one an explosion and that one a bomb, and the place a fighter jet-ghost.

Enter the abyss then and read in the pages that are called faces, read all the varied ages and epochs, from stone to atom, passing by Noah's ship and her sisters, the ones that course through the desert's sands.

Read: The man is a gray lump, with a pointed or rectangular shape. The woman is a red structure, round or bent. The man almost man, and the woman almost woman. You cannot tell if they inhabit clay or if clay inhabits them. But you must find out, you must address your questions to this species that talks about things of an utterly different nature, things like heaven and hell, Satan and God.

And read: Even the sun's rays appear like spider webs weaving the street/
The street that is still woven by priest, colonizer, and capitalist—the three symbols of three European periods that met in Lebanon, surround us in this shelter, and are applauding another accomplishment: the limbs that now fly about as smithereens in the deep darkness of Beirut.

/ . . . And I used to read in the light of a slim candle how space begins to bow, and how all things also bowed. It must have been for a reason, I used to think, to erase the barriers between the visible and the invisible, to mix times together, to mock that upright stick called the sky.

. . . Night with its huge yellow legs is stomping on a yellow earth: This is when I began to blather. I saw terror bring its fog and it began to roof our heads with it in the shelter. And I saw the abyss embrace our days, the abyss through whose cracks I heard the sounds of the nearby sea, and its wrinkled face, and the spots that colored the edges of a horizon that lay on a pillow of foam.

In each of our hearts there was a pulse that nestled itself inside each second. We were like creatures from another nature, sucking on night's blood, not to strengthen ourselves with thought, but so that we can shake the hand of the oncoming dawn.

I return then to the warm companionship of the slim candle, to Cadmus and Electra, to names born under flame, from Gilgamesh to al-Mutannabi, passing by Imruulqais and Abu Tammam, and not forgetting Abu Nawwas; and from Homer to St. John Perse, passing by Heraclitis and Sophocles, Dante and Nietzsche, and not forgetting Rimbaud: the light of an ephemeral candle that becomes an eternity of stars.

The scent of the candle climbs the dark walls, then descends and stretches over the book I had used as a portable pillow.

It is morning: the sun renews its time and life renews its flesh.

THE CHILD RUNNING INSIDE MEMORY

An arch of basil leaves, a bower for doves
windows have flung their doors
      to the hand of   the wind / the fields—
            a village of palm fronds and the ink of seasons.

Thunder's anger and the clouds' kindness raised me there
a village among whose underclothes we lay
and where fig and mulberry whispered what lips were too shy to say.

At the heights of the palms my memory grew.
Here we harvest sumac and here these beans—
We won't go without that sweet spice this afternoon—
Here a child holding two eagles
so that roses greet each other.

At the heights of the palms my memory grew.
Violets came barefoot
and why not
since my friend the grass offered me an arm and I gave it my shirt
           and we were sheltered under the hand of an olive tree.
I have a wind in the book of green and a promise in blue
I keep a book in the sun's purse . . .

At the heights of the palms my memory grew
   a stream of willows, a weeping—
   Is it the jinns playing their music
   or is this the branches' tune? Go on humming
   willow, and let me listen
   and let me see my face wearing yours
      a premonition reading the voice of the water in the silence of stone
      and blood writing on its leaves
      a rain that combs the branches of the trees.

My memory descended
from the heights of the palms /   Peace
   to my friend, the boy running in my memory
   he did not visit me today, did not confide in me
   as was his habit—I surrendered my face
   to his mirrors: Which of us is lost?
   Who is silent, who speaking? His lips
   darken—Does he live there now?

Boy running in my memory,
my bleeding wound is painful but
my body grows and grows strong.
The sea and I share the same death—
I am the lark of sadness, the wolf of joy.
And you, rising in these heights
are you a rainbow or are you another wound?

My memory descended
from the heights of the palms /   Peace
to my look-alike, the boy settled at the bottom of memory.
Are you the force bolting in my pulse, are you the fire?
Peace to you, kind friend
you survived by luck and you renamed the moon
a horse sometimes, and sometimes a horseman.
The sun sistered you and you both built
the house you made of straw
and she played with pebbles like you /   If you'd only given me your hand . . .

And peace
to you trees swaying in my memory—
Am I your utterance or silence, or what the wind carries toward you
from the dust of other trees?
                              If only you'd offer me your hands
if only the horizon, awake all through your sleepless vision,
would tell me what happened in the forest of my days, the winds of memory . . .

At the heights of the palms my memory grew—
          I didn't know that a lover's body is drawn with a swallow's beak
          I didn't know that only madness knows how to love.

For whom is the star letting loose her hair?
The horses of fatigue will meet her by the threshing floor
a road between her eyes and her hands
                              a tent . . .

Is it true? Take me then

           . . . / a pool of sadness and the lakes of night / we dove

           and divided the water's moon.

Yes, it's true

           even the stars dream of living in a hut made of reeds.

Desire Moving Through Maps of Matter

1987

DESIRE MOVING THROUGH MAPS OF MATTER

1.

It came to pass
  knives fall from the sky
  the body lurches forward
  the soul trails behind.

It came to pass
  blacksmiths' hammers knocking inside a skull
    dumbness the erasure of races,—
    writing: an ideological acid
    books: linden trees.

2.

<table>
<tr><td>

Where can I hold my feasts of survival
how can I release my wings
weeping in the cages of language
and how can I live in memory
a bay choked with debris?

</td><td>

(A)

He named the language "woman"
  writing "love"
  and began looking for seashells

in the hoopoe's lexicon
  (the allusion is to elsewhere,
  not Solomon and Sheba's queen)

</td></tr>
</table>

Will a stone or a poppy sprout between my shoulders, will the animals caged inside me escape, will I doze off and betray my limbs, will I make plugs out of dirt to stopper my lungs and lie on the black stone of obedience, will I anoint myself with engine oil and stuff my throat with yes, yes, no, no?

No, I have no country
except for these clouds rising as mist from lakes of poetry.
Shelter me, Dhawd, guard me, Dhawd[1]—
                    my language, my home—
          I hang you like a charm around the throat of this era
          and explode my passions in your name
          not because you are a temple
          not because you are my father or mother
          but because I dream of laughter, and I weep through you
          so that I translate my insides
                    and cling to you as I tremble as my sides shudder like windows
     shaken by a wind let loose from God's fingers.

It is through you that I turn into a breath
                    that falls from the sky's lips
                    and blows into the earth's genitals.
This is how I embrace you and say again:
                    You are the body that names tomorrow
                    and it is on you that the dice of history are tossed.

3.
To make a mirror that deserves me
and to see myself reflected in it

to shape a space wide enough to contain my horrors
         maybe I'll put on a shirt with ripped sleeves
         or walk in tattered socks and shoes
         maybe I'll slit a cloud's vein
         and sate my thirst
         maybe I'll whisper "Home" and only the history
         of a dervish fated to die will be revealed to me
         maybe I'll cover his grave with my voice
or try to uproot the Eiffel Tower
and replace it with a sapling of Damascene jasmine
or maybe I'll invite Adam back to earth
so that he can build a house for his beloved on earth
and call his children home.

Now the sun combs the hair of dusk as the bars of Paris rise up like the Virgin in
      her ascent—
                           I summon angels and ambulances—
      I turn into water and flow in the pool of my sorrows
      or
      I become a horizon and climb the heights of desire.

      I know that we die only once   and are many times reborn
      and I know that death is only useful if we live it through.
      I know that the hereafter is this rose
         this woman
         and that a human face is the other side of the sky.

I know that my skies will rise from the Edens of Earth
cloud by cloud.
Welcome to history, to its specks of dust!
How can a mortal despair
when the wind is his road?

4.
To my relief there's no way to meet Richard the Lionheart or Louis XIV
or even Napoleon.
Dressed in fog I was free
and I enjoyed seeing dogs lying on women's breasts.
I don't remember seeing a single star dance
or read or walk like the stars of my childhood.
I have had to imagine the stars of my village Qassabin
guiding me as I wandered the streets
listening to people's lamentations flow
as the Seine refused them reprieve.
He came to the café (the Deux Magots, I believe)
and with him came the church of St. Germain-des-Près,
a sky with a torn spine.
Jean Genet came to convince him to reconcile with God
(if only to discover the hell of heaven)
An earth, that had no wish to look at the sky, came.
Sorcerers came to read the stars
and voices from the Third/Arab world
heavy with messages from the beyond.

(B)

[(How can I convince al-Ghazzali[2]   (in Orly
to see his soul   the Third World is a crippled elephant
with Nietzsche's light?   falling with a parachute and saying:
I'll remind him: "Paris is allying itself with other planets
You've been traveling toward the world   learning the revolution of the sun"
since its creation   then suddenly, inexplicably
but you have not arrived)]   the elephant dissolves becoming a river of
        blood
      flooding the houses and shops.)

5.

In the café
I ignore the noise.
I read Nietzsche and imagine him as a flood—
        Yes, I should yield to the flood of meaning
        bow like a sunflower, befriend the sun
        or surrender to the lilies of desire
        that float on the lake of my body
        and empty myself to become the child
        I had wanted to be in the future.

6.

(C)

Did you see the poet, his face transparent

                in daylight, his feet

                    lost in night?

Did you see him lean his back against

the light, trying to set water on fire?

Did you see his papers turn into crowns in

    the wind?

(. . . in a place shaped like a windmill

where time is a wall of words—

the mortar holding them together is ink

—There's a solitary statue of Don

            Quixote made of paper

a solitary statue of his horse—

The air is a cloak

falling from a leaden sky)

Sex assumes the throne:

Wolves, set to ambush their prey wrapped in the fur

                of words,

leap out of the fables of La Fontaine.[3]

Beggars lie on the bare ground cushioning their heads with empty bottles.

             Some of them criticize Mallarmé

             some dream of Rimbaud

             some read de Sade.

The Sixteenth Arrondissement is a forest of bobbing heads; its museums

            are made of sexual organs and can be found everywhere.

Ash covers the surface of space, vocal cords strum like

        a warning:

Rimbaud

how can I cross this white world

              I whose body is prophecy

and whose house is the Sahara?
And how can I explain the light from the beyond
              with this world's words?
I must, must . . .
make my own morals
write an inaugural poem for my death.

7.

(D)

They're preparing their atomic dust/   (. . . this is what is told about contagion
we repeat the prayer of the dead.   and how time's ovaries turned to rot.
From water to sand, from sand to snow   Machines cook humans in a purple soup,
the whole world is a fish, caught.   an East equipped with gods, invisible to us
                                                   except for their cloven hooves
                                                and a West that sees only guts and jaws
                                                as it collapses beneath mountains of
                                                electronic grain)

The East is a wound, its politics pus
and it will rain on the West
              and it will rain on houses where the grass
              tainted with diesel and uranium grows,
              a rain of blackness and mud.

8.
Oh, monsieur's mistress is pissing on the heads of Les Invalides;
monsieur's dog is shitting on the pillow of l'Arc de Triomphe.

9.

A dead man gives, a dead man takes,
and the one who holds my soul in his hand
and the one whose soul I hold in my hand
their voices converge   in a chorus of words
echoing over the edge of a cliff.

       Is this world other
       than what I see?

And you, supreme roving planets, moved
by the flick of a finger
      I invite you to this feast of disaster
      history spiced by cooks who garnish plagues
and where all labor is a sword spearing water.

Here where the left builds its nests
      and the right lays its eggs
      I see time rise in hills of white powder
      while I measure the heights

(E)

Black clouds coming from all
directions converge
the last remaining feasts reach their
end and the atom, a fly buzzing
and creeping on the forehead of time—
Oh that secret bread
that nourishes electric rats!

(F)

The Western poet
must also learn
how to weep among ruins
to write on sand
and learn how to bind
balm and poison
to solve
what cannot be solved
      and learn
how to praise the wind

(G)

"What women! What books!"
exclaims the revolutionary
      as he begins to disappear
      like a dot on a line

where dream birds soar
as the mosque of the Fifth Arrondissement
cleanses itself for worship
and enters the whiteness of prayer
In the morning while Boulevard St. Michel coughs
out its innards and falls in a stampede of passersby
I enjoy watching the sky slip between my shoulders
and a stray cat meow into the ear of the wind.
I can detect only two types of people in Paris
one still dreaming, lost among the paths of May '68,
one sprawled on sixteenth-century rugs.
How can I reconcile the ashes of Paris
      with our bleeding sun?
How can I reconcile the shores of the sea
      we share while I contend with
      the emperors of futility
      and dethrone the sultans of sense?
How can I reconcile the Eiffel Tower
      with the basilisk in the Place de la
      Concorde—
for the tower is cold and half dead
      and the basilisk a beautiful lover
      standing tall and upright like an Alif.
Nowhere has the bed of mankind seen
      a more beautiful nude.

in a footnote shrinking in a corner.
Is your throat clogged with cement?
Did your flood ebb in this café?
And the West, what can it give your
      desert
except more sand
and why is your voice unheard
except when it rises
from the reeds that sprout
around springs that still gush
from your fertile land?
      O mysterious guest
take no offense when I tell you
"work before death comes to claim you
and die not like a moth
but like a rose"

10.

Paris   (H)

your light deceives me   1. (say that time has come to feast

      (it crouches on the ground,   that life is a pebble that time cooks

it walks leaning on crutches)   that death is life's raw meat)

should I ask a magic carpet to show me around?   2. (say that words are the offspring

                               of paper,

                   prophecies made by the wind)

I take off from Monmartre, from the sill of

       Sacré-Coeur.

I land in an oval plate adorned by the lamb

       of Jerusalem.

I recognize Michel Simon

who raised goats in his room

I see people like M. Bisson[4]

and his wife who groom animals

and hold their funerals.

I visit a secret cemetery (secret

for fear of grave robbers)

and sit in cafés that remind me of the café of the blind

       in the Palais Royal arcade

       filled with tired people   (I)

       exhaling their hours like cotton plumes.   He sees the sky crucified

                                on an image of André Breton

                                and holds a star

                                deceived by the gleam of surrealism

                                and lets it weep in his arms

Paris

    I have assembled your severed limbs

    inside of me

    and I have given you

    a new body.

                                          (J)

(The soul is a wordless ghost   The phoenix is not a belly;

only the body can speak)   it is imagination

                                    So what is the use of knocking

                                    on Karl Marx's head as if he's a door

                                    and climbing him like a ladder

I am now tracing the footsteps of the hunchback   as if desire can live without arms,

    not the one in whose arms   as if the dream remains a

                                        frozen river?

    Notre Dame slept   He gave this speech in the confusion

    but the one who can be seen   of Bastille Square (and listening to it

    every day, that ghost who creeps   were Saint-Just, Robespierre, and

    along the pavements of St. Michel   Danton

    and on whom night forms an arch when   along with all the rest)[5]

    it reaches toward the Sixteenth Arrondissement,   A voice cried out, "Death to

                                        the void

    where the male body is a zoo   that swallows voices and souls!"

    and the female a garden of androgynous plants.   Amen! other voices replied

"Ghost," I whisper, then turn to Nerval[6] and ask

    "Was the rope as soft as you'd wished?"

Verlaine,

look, poetry's arms extend all the way to the Opéra's

dome; they're holding a golden harp.
Oh, look again, it's breaking into pieces where
your corpse passed heading to its final abode.

Your "feasts of love" rode along the carriage that took
Berlioz to Montmartre cemetery—their neighing farewell.

"Ghost," I whisper again and walk toward St. Germain
　　　　to greet Apollinaire: "Hello, dear ghost, hello to you!"

11.

The Eiffel Tower　　　　　　　**Notre Dame**　　　　　　**The Louvre**
(I must be dreaming. The Eiffel Tower has disappeared.
　　　　　　I see the Louvre heading toward the eastern shore of the Mediterranean
　　　　　　as if to follow in Alexander's footsteps.
　　　　　　Notre Dame falls asleep as it prays　　　　it taps the shoulders
　　　　　　of the sky and rests its head on the pillow of its dreams.

The Eiffel Tower　　　　　　　**Notre Dame**　　　　　　**The Louvre**
　　　The Mosque of the Fifth Arrondissement

(Is a statue going to convince me that a Western virgin was the first to become pregnant
　　　　　　　　with reason,
and who was it that once said these famous words: "Now the stomach has spoken,
　　　　　　and we deem that East and West are mortal enemies
　　　　　　and dust shall be their judge!"
I look at the faces and think, "There's nothing inanimate in the inanimate, nothing
　　　　　　inanimate anywhere except in man.")

Notre Dame   **The Mosque of the Fifth Arrondissement**

Weep now, angels of hell

there will be no more visitors for you to burn and relish   in flocks and schools.

All the animals will enter Paradise, the speaking and the dumb.

12.

          It has happened at last—

               the memory of races shall explode—

      Abu Nawwas   **Baudelaire**

Among the human clan some can speak   Congealed angels of Notre Dame

      but never utter a word.   need female shapes

      They are not mute   in order to walk on air

      they have no defects

                                air that refuses to budge

In a desert ripe for invasion   unless you blow it from your soul

war erupts   where women are broken jugs

among this one and that and this   lying in beds beneath

not to liberate anyone   the Seine's vaults—bridges are their

but to preserve slavery   floating dreams

A hand now disrobes the air   Here the robotic mind wraps itself

and dresses it in clean clothes   in Krishna's robes and the black minotaur

                                sleeps in the arms of a white woman

My body leads me to a house   Angels of wisdom flee their prisons

that I know is not my body   to embrace the angels of desire

                                in a nebula of signs

It is a beautiful night   where each sign is a dictionary
that melts and disappears among my clothes
where God too is drenched
in the sweat of our time

It has happened—

Explode now, memory of races—

Al-Mutannabi   **Hugo**

The creed hammers its nails   An age—a brewery from which
prey chased by mice . . .   the victims' blood
                                                               and the murderer's saliva
Creatures with chicken heads   pour out together
and the bodies of giants
in kingdoms-concubines . . .   Chaos where things mix—
                                                               animals made of straw run
Someone holds a spear   chased by blind infants
with a head on its blade
a symbol of his power   heads like Orpheus'
pieces of corpses and skulls   that swim in smoke
commas and motions   not in water

Fables pulse vein to vein   In a scream that no lips have released
in a history wound in a reel for safekeeping   you see hands flailing without bodies
(Praise be to camphor and celluloid!)

Feet walk in tandem, both to the left   Workers return at night to their shacks
                    both to the right   carrying twigs which are only
                                                               the thighs of the jobless

Does the body adhere to the state of the soul?
I ask a man in Beirut wearing red slippers
and riding a locust who screamed her refrain at me:
Vanity, all is vanity.
No, no
my body loves this pale sky
My dreams swerve off their course.

I imagine that creature making a noose out of his face
walking along the banks of the Euphrates and the Nile
at the same time.
He hugs the shores of the Seine, Hudson and Thames.
He sleepwalks so that he can feel his limbs.

Praise be to ambiguity!
Should I wait and harvest other seeds instead?

13.

My passion is sprouting seeds secretly, from Heraclitus and Nietzsche
because among my sorrows laurel leaves still rustle
and between my shoulders a sail has set forth
(I had seen it once on the Mediterranean near the island of Arwad
but my memory could not guard its name)
because I am chasing the head of an atom
coming out of an electric cave
wrapped around itself like an onion
spilling the sounds of clerical trumpets
and still attached to the trunk of the sixteenth century

because all you need now, to make the body of a man
                    are the legs of an ant and the head of a locust
                            (and for his soul place anything
                            that you can buy from the souq)
because the powers of the sky bow before the throne of Joan d'Arc
                    and because her sword still drips with water
                    that heals lepers
because the stomach of this age is still Nero's
because when I read about freedom in this world
                    I find that I'm chasing a three-colored rat
                    chasing a cat with two tails and three wings.

14.
Is Paris's body drying up? I asked myself
in Champs de Mars as I greeted a planet
                    that soon turned into a clump of mimosa fleece
                    around which the stars of speech began to orbit—
                    (they were small, the size of Marie Antoinette's buttocks)
The trees did not believe the flowers
and the flowers were suspicious of the sun.
The wind did not give a care
and the dust clapped its hands.
While looking at the Eiffel Tower
I saw a girl carry it away in her arms
(it was almost like a Lewis Carroll story, but not exactly)
The faces around me were shaped like clouds that changed color
the heads were neither lunar nor solar
but from a strange planet.

I find it difficult to describe
(I'll ask Littré about it)[7]
Oh, what paradoxes! They're the only things that make sense.
What contradictions that we can imagine no harmony without!
My musings ended and I turned to Paris again,
                    Maybe when I dive into the innards of nature
                    chanting the names of your streets:
Waterfall Street, Brook Street, Poplar Street
Chestnut Street, Cherry Street, Mulberry Street
Plum Street, Fig Street, Rose Street, Linden Street
(and I won't forget Mouzaïa Street with its ring of Arabic)—
maybe then I'll tuck your vowels into my name
while the consonants continue their heavenly sleep
or maybe I'll weave a fine rug out of them so that no French poet,
not even Francis Ponge, can tell it apart from a wing!

15.
She says, it is so
I say, so be it . . .
I toss my pens into a gash on the face of the moon,
I place my memories in a wrinkle on the Seine's neck.
Run, river, take the dust and its seasons away
and don't forget the river that runs between you and yourself.
Preserve your femininity that appears as your masculine,
preserve the voice inside that had perfected you.
Flow, Seine
in currents that make silt out of humans and other forms of debris—

I see the Seine flowing
   carrying Europe's moss-slathered bells

I see the Seine flowing—
    in its current horses from the Middle Ages
    chariots from the Renaissance, modern
       marionettes
Baudelaire's voice, Lautréamont's, Nerval's
Hugo's, Rimbaud's, Mallarmé's and Picasso's.

It flows, and in its current
revolutions and history
break into crumbs.

She says, it is so
and I say, so be it . . .
   Flow on, river
   let the world's antipodes sit in your lap.
   Give them the last inhale.

Water is desire—
   the divers who invented desire and lust
   keep the banks apart.

(K)
Time arrives with its beasts
How does it tame them?
Time arrives with its abysses
How is it reflected in them?
Time arrives with its guillotines
and everything begins to tremble
Time, your name
sticks in the throat
a kernel of nausea

(L)
(Life wilts in between man's footsteps—
Is this why he treats it
as if it is a sign of his impending
    death?
Is this why he never stops asking
"Will the world fall asleep
in beds made for murder?")

16.

It's my desire that's flowing
        on maps of matter now.
        Every speck of time is now open
        like sexual organs on the beds of space.

On my morning walks
from 116 Lourmel Street
to 1 Miollis Street, I read
the ocean's book
in a drop of water.
I touch a light that lurches
like a plough and I discover how
a poet remains an infant
though he is as old as the horizon.
That's why I do not hesitate to say:
"I and the Other
are I"

and time is only a basket
to collect poetry.

I meet Rimbaud unexpectedly
and we renew our pact:
The veil is a light—
West is another name of East.

(M)

Neither East nor West belongs
to God   (Forgive me, Goethe.)
North is sinking in the ice of memory,
and South, whenever it imagines itself
cured of a disease, contracts another
and consoles itself
by repeating this ditty:
Joy is Sorrow's
closest friend

(N)

Why do his feet know the Seine
better than they know
the Tigris or the Barada?[8]
What a fool! He loves mankind
   more than he loves the Earth
and the Earth more than his homeland

17.

No, the body is not a pelican's or a water lily's
but under my eyelashes Ophelia sleeps.
She discovers me by mistake and my dreams
turn into rapturous lakes.

Now, as Hamlet listens,
I tell myself:
Be wise
and remember that love and suffering
come from the same household.
Stop worrying
about day and night
moon and sun.

It is true, as Hamlet has shown
that love often breaks out in war
and that the body sometimes needs
a storm to rearrange its parts.
So tonight in Paris I watch over the streets
as they wander about like a flock of animals
and I see fountains of flame
erupt from the thighs of towers.
I mumble:
Nothing renders me clear as this obscurity
or maybe, nothing obscures me like this clarity.

(O)

I—The Seine hasn't flowed East, not yet
(this is not an allusion to the "holy
blessings" that Goethe's praised
in his *Divan*: the turban, the tent
the curved sword, the dirge)
This river's waters have yet to mix
like the Euphrates'
with the planet's light

II—(We haven't raised
another pillar of wisdom
to help us build spaceships
to take us, not to other planets
but to our own homes
or help us build winged creatures
that would take us, the poor of this earth
who dream of pilgrimage
and of circling their idols.
No, we haven't turned the wind
into a perfect roll of the dice.)

III—How can he be so calm?—
a fish in the waters
of his era
How can he live in a body drained
of its substance?
How can he take apart a real body
made of his own words
a body held up
by the columns
of bodiless languages?

This is I—
from among my race, I waft like perfume
              from a dying rose.
I move, slow-surge, I spread
and like a bee I make my own honey.
This life is cold
not even a wound
nothing but machinery
crowding the fields
of human breath.
There is no day or night
only an endless thread of disconnected moments.
The outside is no home for me
the inside confines me.
        Among my race I waft like perfume
        from a dying rose.
I have no wish to name.
I want to be exalted like light.
I do not want to hold fast any longer.
I want to run alongside the wind.

THE CRADLE

(Excerpt)

"Twenty for the price of ten . . . next to nothing, next to nothing," a boy repeats, repeats his
pitch, tossing the threads of his voice toward the Bazz and Nuhas markets, tilting his small
mirror toward the sky and letting its light wander among the shoppers' feet   In an
aromatic storm the markets intersect, arteries and veins in this body that is neither fact nor
dream

Sanaa[9] I take you between my arms   we walk with men who lift
the day to create a parasol of sadness   with women who carry on their shoulders anxieties
the color of raisins   their feet bear only one desire—
to be kissed by the wind

Lanterns   the Arwa mosque leans on Sheba's[10] calculations,   candles
that have gone out but still bear a spark of divine revelation   I read their secrets
scroll by scroll   I hold back the allusions and the details   There's a
   storm building up   I ask you, candles,
where are those who stay up all night? Whose finger is on the trigger now?

The entrance to the market /   Slow down, this is not water, but blood   This is not a
   wall but
the backbone of a man who once said, "NO"
The end of the market /   A woman, an ebony planet in the ether of sighs
                                        —"Will we ever meet?"

I let night sleep on the doorstep, while a star was about to break into my room to recite its
body to me
The markets were rocking in waves when I recalled what Hamdani[11] had said:
"No woman in the world can match a beauty from Sanaa"

I speak to Sanaa and walk around Aden
Fishermen draw their shadows on the sea   city folks and Bedouins
They press the body of matter to speak and shake the shore's memory   Their dreams are
horses that never stop neighing . . .

A mare of desire—
History, your light and skin play with our desires   but your sword is
rusted and we are a stone of want . . .   And stone, we chose you from among the
desert's treasures . . .   Because of you we took "splitting" as our name   with
you we broke up   and through you we firmed up and became welded to each
other . . .   To us you are water's brother
(stone is solid water   water is liquid stone)

I say Aden and Sanaa   and I harbor this cradle-boat
" . . . We are Asia and Africa washed in the waters of the future, dressed in the straw of
beginnings . . . We are not made of metal, we are made of man."

I say Aden and Sanaa and I mean this cradle/boat
—How can Ghamdan[12] remain a young man for thousands of years?
—How can I answer when I "have fortified Ghamdan with mysteries?"
(*Ikleel al-Hamdani*)[13]

Sanaa, a while ago I saw an image of you and you've changed already   you are a dress
opening, lifting softly like an eyelid—how strange this mixture that weaves this moment /

Silk Market

    A woman of the jinn of Sheba   Her dress (feathers, embroidery, silk fuzz)

    Pleasures   barefoot   her sleeves are birds

    A sign board: "The rising of her motions   like female horses

            They would not relent except for neighing and frolic"

                                        (Belquis)[14]

Grain Market

    An engraving: "This world is never sweet to my eye

            and what is not sweet to the eye is not sweet to the mouth"

Gold Market

    A sign board: "Everything that is near is broad"

    An engraving: "The wise one renounces life as if death is at hand

              and works for eternity"

Silver Market

    An engraving: "The artisan is conscientious so that he betters himself

             He excels at his work to better the world"

Qat Market

    Parchment: "My hands reach for what my eyes do not see"

Spice Market
      Parchment: "What I want leaves me, and becomes what I do not want"

Raisin Market
      Engraving: "I am the shepherd of the quarter; if I drink the whole place
                      gets lost"

Henna Market
      A sign board: "What is the color of God?"
                            (Belquis)

I have a lineage in the soil of Yemen
     I descend with her to the beginnings to better discover what comes:
         Anemones
     baskets of grapes rise from the soil of the hills . . . breasts in a hurry to be
                               caressed
     and behind them the ceramics of the ages disintegrate   Thanks to life and to
                                 her
     dual night   Thanks to the wisdom of a stone who believes it is my friend
     And you, be sure to stay warm, my secrets.   Or do I need to cover you too?
Sanaa,   the wind carries me   I am beginning to master the speech of birds
the speech of all things
     The mountains walk with me and the jinns stay behind . . .

I have a lineage in the soil of Yemen
     on streets that begin to take on features when facing the light of
         day
     in night that wears the stars like necklaces and earrings

in the words that laugh and weep in the depths of everything
in an estrangement that overwhelms my depths
in hands that weave weeping into tents of dream
in an unknown I plant myself within
where the stump of creation had taken root
I say I have a lineage
      in the soil of Yemen
          I belong to it
              a country without age
                as if it were
                    the face of God

THE JOY IMPLEMENT
(Excerpt)

Sit down

Let me tell you the story of smoke

This joy implement lives alone in the house of words

    She is embraced by a reed that links water to fire

    and in the bottom of its pole

    where a specter of narcissus floats—the Arab name for the flower of the self—

    where history dreams peacefully

    under a crescent moon shaped like a pillow on which the reed pipe

        leans

    The reed is different, and its body does not belong to the

            moon

      but to someone else

            Move your lips   it could be you

      The reed ends in a globe (also called coconut, pipe, and pomegranate)

      On its back is a colorful garden of designs and engravings

        Inside it is a dove holding up a lake, almost black, that I cannot see

        but I think I see behind it or over it a mountain of smoke

      and I see maidens reclined on sofas

      One side of the reed is linked to where the smoke is distilled (the tobacco

        chamber)   and where there is a tip

     that will remind of breast and suckling once you place your lips on it

   You will ask yourself: Am I not this mixture of fire, water, and air?

Then you will enjoy whispering to yourself: You too are part of this fabric that weaves earth and sky . . .

The water inside the globe is burning with my sadnesses   But my sadnesses are dressed in silence   And in my face nothing can be read except the cloud-cover of questions   And when that red hue besieges my eyes, the fabric that surrounds the reed, the one that my heart refuses to see except as blue or lavender,   I say, "each color has an inside and an outside"   Otherwise life would have choked on the inks of nature, and space would have been too narrow for the wind   I say, the joy implement too is a neighborhood in the city of my pleasures   And what things there are in this neighborhood!   Some of its alleyways are like braids or streams and some of them bear a great craving as if their embers burned with God's fire

A light seeps from the water in the oval glass   It walks among my limbs   It dances behind my shoulders

My neck is a ladder climbing the horizon and my head is a blue sun

Celebrating Vague-Clear Things

1988

CELEBRATING CHILDHOOD

Even the wind wants
to become a cart
pulled by butterflies.

I remember madness
leaning for the first time
on the mind's pillow.
I was talking to my body then
and my body was an idea
I wrote in red.

Red is the sun's most beautiful throne
and all the other colors
worship on red rugs.

Night is another candle.
In every branch, an arm,
a message carried in space
echoed by the body of the wind.

The sun insists on dressing itself in fog
when it meets me:
Am I being scolded by the light?

Oh, my past days—
they used to walk in their sleep
and I used to lean on them.

Love and dreams are two parentheses.
Between them I place my body
and discover the world.

Many times
I saw the air fly with two grass feet
and the road dance with feet made of air.

My wishes are flowers
staining my days.

I was wounded early,
and early I learned
that wounds made me.

I still follow the child
who still walks inside me.

Now he stands at a staircase made of light
searching for a corner to rest in
and to read the face of night again.

If the moon were a house,
my feet would refuse to touch its doorstep.

They are taken by dust
carrying me to the air of seasons.

I walk,
one hand in the air,
the other caressing tresses
that I imagine.

A star is also
a pebble in the field of space.

He alone
who is joined to the horizon
can build new roads.

A moon, an old man,
his seat is night
and light is his walking stick.

What shall I say to the body I abandoned
in the rubble of the house
in which I was born?
No one can narrate my childhood
except those stars that flicker above it
and that leave footprints
on the evening's path.

My childhood is still
being born in the palms of a light
whose name I do not know
and who names me.

Out of that river he made a mirror
and asked it about his sorrow.
He made rain out of his grief
and imitated the clouds.

Your childhood is a village.
You will never cross its boundaries
no matter how far you go.

His days are lakes,
his memories floating bodies.

You who are descending
from the mountains of the past,
how can you climb them again,
and why?

Time is a door
I cannot open.
My magic is worn,
my chants asleep.

I was born in a village,
small and secretive like a womb.
I never left it.
I love the ocean not the shores.

CELEBRATING DEATH

Death arrives from the back
even when it comes before us.
Only life confronts.

The eye is a road
and the road is an intersection.

A child plays with life,
an old man leans on it.

The tongue rusts from excess of speech,
and the eye dries from lack of dreams.

Wrinkles—
grooves on the face,
potholes in the heart.

A body—half doorstep,
half incline.

His head is a butterfly
with a single wing.

The sky reads you
after death writes you.

The sky has two breasts;
from them all people suckle
every moment, every place.

The human being is a book
life reads continuously,
and death reads in an instant,
and only once.

What about this city?
In it dawn appears like a walking stick
in a darkness named Time.

Spring came to the garden of the house,
laid down his suitcases
and started giving them to the trees
under a rain falling from his arms.
Why is the poet always mistaken?
Spring gives him its leaves
and he gives them to ink.

Our existence is a slope
and we live to climb it.

I congratulate you, sand.
You are the only one who can pour
water and mirage
into the same bowl.

CELEBRATING ABU TAMMAM

Excerpts from the Memoirs of Abu Tammam, *a novel by Mihyar of Damascus*[1]

I. Between Jassim and Baghdad

1.

Here's space taking, evaporating, me:

>I move toward someone else.

>Night has horses, and the day is a horseman.

2.

There, my senses are traveling,

and are about to pass me by.

And here my voice is about to rise from the throat

>>of the wind.

3.

Trees are words

and light writes the distances.

4.

I read.

>The innards of matter approach me,

>and the limbs of time fill up with signals.

5.

Here I am, and Jassim is moving further from me.

>My body is splitting away

>and my head is running to catch up with it.

I lie under a willow tree.

>Why does she refuse to unbutton her dress,

>she, who never leaves water?

6.

I rove,

listen to the wind moaning in my memory.

I surprise the palms strolling with my steps.

7.

Time in Baghdad is not old or young.

Time in Baghdad is a flower.

I do not know how to grasp it

and not make it wilt.

8.

The stones here wane like faces

and dust drags its cape to the gulf.

In every direction

a palm tree awaits

her share of pollen dust.

9.

Let this sheet of paper

describe what it saw on the banks of Barada.[2]

10.

It's Baghdad's sun—

why do I guide the horizon to it

and it guides flight toward me?

11.

The nation? Yes,

on the condition that it too belongs to me.

II. The Story of a Day

1.

Clouds toil for the future
and rain must prove the virtue of that labor.

2.

Ships carry the sea.
Seas
groan under the weight of vessel-dreams.

3.

Frogs wear shoes made of water.
Birds migrate wearing their most beautiful shirts.

4.

The wind falls in the traps it sets for others.

5.

A princess, the sun sits in the lobby of the horizon.
Friends gather,
spiders and birds,
royal butterflies and worker bees,
crickets and lizards,
guests to one desire,
no difference between cicadas and lizards.
The sun rides her carriage
and her guests rule the realm.

6.

From the branches of this tree a voice rises
for the wind to carry
and not know.

7.

When the poet writes
he becomes a lyre
in the hands of language.

8.

Because I am often silent
words seep out of my flesh.

9.

Time, you who are stitched to me,
my poetry embroiders you
and my voice is embellishments and decorations.

10.

A body becomes a lily and sleeps in water;
a body rules over a lake of fire.

III. Questions I Did Not Answer

1.

In all you have written
you have only left us another shape of night.
Is this why
there was nothing in your body except light?

2.

You wanted through language to know yourself and the world.
        You provoked the thing against the name
and the name against the thing.
They are still wrestling, searching and not finding.
Why after all this
do you seem to know
only the things that have no name?

3.

Between your steps and space,
letters written by a stranger.
The letter "Mim"
you called "Ha"
and the letter "Alif"
you called "Ya."
Why, and how, do you maintain
this invisible history?

IV. Questions Posed by Mihyar of Damascus

1.

I descend countless steps toward your pediment.
   Sometimes I imagine I reach it
   but quickly I discover
   there are more steps going down—
where do you live, O near one?

2.

Your poetry was a prophecy that preceded your steps.
Is this why, O grand mountain,
you flutter around us like a wing?

3.

You turn words into pinnacles.
You stay at the highest point
where descent is impossible
and where you wait for fate to reach you.
Is it not heading for you now
scratching the roads with its eyelashes?

V. The Art of Poetry

1.

A sheet of paper is the letter $(\jmath)^3$
flying circles, searching for its pillow.

2.

The seasons are not four.
A week is not seven days.
A year is more than it is,
and less.

3.

The pen writes the paper's trembling
and paper writes the darkness that melts in light.
Whenever the pen wanted to write the end,
the words led it to the beginning.

4.

The sun washes the body of matter,
and a creature hiding
is now ready to pounce.

5.

In the dialogue between trees and wind,
the lips of the branches
surrender to the kiss of dust.

6.

Flowers dispense their nectar
in bottles the air makes.

7.

A butterfly is a suitcase
bearing colors.

8.

A picture is a lantern,
a rose-colored artery
in the body of speech.

9.

In words lit by images,
each seems a person
standing and dreaming.

10.

I enter the throbbing darkness
to learn how to welcome light.

11.

Transparency is also a veil.
The sun
is itself a shadow.

I. Childhood

1.

His childhood was a friendship between his cane and the road. Darkness was a memory for his steps. Since then he has joined word and space, combined their faces. He knew also that death was his sole paradise.[4]

2.

He did not walk for pleasure, but to inquire. A certain music accompanied him, a music rising from trees played by air. Wherever he went he felt he was falling into traps where he wished to remain.

3.

He never cared to know where the wind was headed.

II. Days

1.

Say, the place is desolate.
Say, the world is clay, and humans are projects for humanity.
And here space is shackled in the chains of night.

2.

Damn this filthy, endless motion,
this four-legged child.

3.

How strange, this age, this vaporous shirt.
How strange this sky,
a roof supported by spears.

4.

Dust leans on the body.

History: bubbles on a lake of blood.

5.

I am not the lost one.

The planet I live on is.

6.

I merge with the nonexistent

to rotate in the entirety of the whole.

7.

Happiness is born an old man

and dies a child.

8.

Woe to the forest that kills

the wolf and the lamb

in one celebration.

9.

The world is a pot,

and words are its ruinous bottom.

10.

An hour of insomnia rules the earth.

     Blood coagulates

     and pain is the scent of time.

11.

Here is melancholy

     sitting at home secluded from others

     not finding a face

     that fits its features.

12.

Death, you are more truthful to me than my tongue,

gentler than my body, tell me

to whom do I belong? How can I

reshape myself, and move in different ways?

This is an impotent mood.

This is a crippled nature.

13.

Between a dawn rising with the face of a locust

and an evening falling with the eyes of a bat,

their sadness runs on paper

and mine runs with the streams.

14.

Who guides this dust? Who mixes the eye with straw?

I doubted.

I suspected.

Is it because I had the most premonitions that I have become the most confused?

15.

I ask ash and smile,

do you really think there is fire under you?

What wisdom is guiding you, old man?

16.

What right does the chaff have

to refuse the long march

back to the grain?

17.

Summer broke its jugs and winter's clock has stopped.

There are sparks of spring

rising from autumn's cart.

18.

I am not surprised by the man who grows like a mushroom and falls apart like moss.
I am not surprised by the victim
who learns from his killer.

19.

I trust neither sun nor moon,
and the stars are not pillows or dreams.
I trust ash,

> where trees are fright
> and stone is smoke
> where fatigue ruffles its wings over the earth.

20.

Say the dead rear the living
and the world is the garden's death.

III. Conversation

—What have you seen, blind one?
—How little the world is, how little I am.
—What have you seen, blind one?
—Fire hides even when its flames attack the stars.
—What have you seen, blind one?
—Who should I trust, when my self is the betrayer?
—What have you seen, blind one?
—As if my speech is the messenger of the wind.
—What have you seen, blind one?
—They exalted the heartless, repeated their lies,

> and when asked if the lie was truth, they said, "Indeed!"

—What have you to say, blind one?

—"The body is a rag dragged on earth.
Walls of the world, support me."

IV. Letters

    1.

You were blind,

but now you are a future.

      And here you are reading roads and space,

          trees and fields,

            and reading people.

    2.

You are enigmatic. You say the thing and its opposite. But you do not contradict yourself. And you do not care for so-called facts, but for discovering paths that lead to the void, tossing your reader into nothingness. It is not a system, but the air of the world and its movements and flavor. Is this why you create only what perplexes and destroys?

The only alliance you have made with the world is the bond of writing.
From writing you took your road to meet death. And writing is your death wish, a desire that flows in words the way blood flows in veins. Are you trying to tell us that writing is breathing an air that is death?

Death is silence. Writing is preparation for this silence and a celebration of it. We master the art of silence to recognize the face of death, to learn how to die.

Writing is the body for that which has no body. It does not lead to any certainty, but to doubt and confusion. Endless questioning. Another kind of death.

Is this why you speak
like the sea forming waves,
the way the desert's body re-creates itself?
Is this why you are two selves
that always disagree?

V. Explanations

1.

This is not a world that ends. It is already finished since it is essentially death.

2.

Death negates meaning. Death itself no longer has a meaning.

3.

Life produces death, which is its essence.

4.

Life uproots death to survive.
It is death yesterday, now, and tomorrow.

5.

The human being is a process of continuous death.

6.

Death is a human body,
and annihilation is its home.

7.

Death is separation. The greatest happiness is in not being born, in remaining the unit
of origin.

8.

Life is ailment, and death is recovery.
Death is water for this human narcissus.

Another Alphabet

1994

IN THE EMBRACE OF ANOTHER ALPHABET

In the embrace of an alphabet that embraces the earth . . . Qassiyun stays awake
                                        and I rise from sleep.
I write and read and say words to abnegation: not poetry, not prose,
                                        bring on frankincense!
The sun resides inside me   Night, offer me your shadows now

Haven't you learned your lesson? Incense smoke
                        fills your house, dear lover
Air is now blowing like a cough in the throats of space
—Let me create a talisman for my condition
—I can lift you higher, lover, but who will heal you afterward?
—I will tell the whirlwinds of desire that my body has forests that suit its winds

           * He left his solitude and entered exile
           * A few steps always separate him
           from the front. As soon as he reaches it he finds himself behind
           it again
           * He has no childhood; poetry is his childhood
           * This wine is from the liver's dust, not from the vine
           * Damascus will not live on unless it rebuilds the sky

Gates

In a morning lifted by wounds, a neighborhood of Damascus escaped the walls of the city and strolled the orchards of Zainabiya. It said, "I will never return. I have named myself Qissaʻa"

He came

he settled in this neighborhood, in the basement of a cement tower . . .

He spread a bed for dreams that evaporated in the steam of bathhouses he'd read about:

Musk Bathhouse	Rose Bathhouse	Bathhouse of the Beautiful
Chain Bathhouse	Eyebrow Bathhouse	Waterpipe Bathhouse
	Qaishani Bathhouse	Queen Bathhouse

and these are among the most beautiful names.

— Al-shaddad?[1] Is it another bathhouse?

— It's a paste, a bather uses to massage her skin

ginger and cinnamon   oil and peepal leaves

pomegranate syrup, eggs, and myrtle

Some add other contents, harbors for the body's waves

His cellar seemed like a hovel bleeding,

a cave shaking and swaying about to collapse upon itself.

* Does truth always follow departure?

* Will the world be more beautiful, if it becomes free of ugliness?

* Is blood made for anything, but blood?

* Is writing also a sand clock?

* Is impudence the only flower to which the wind bends?

* Are severed fingers the only ones who know how to weld

history's limbs?

* Should loyalty be to ideas or to their creation?
* Is it a crime here to have a name?
* Is life here a pilgrimage to death?
* Does the veil Damascus wears reveal the city to him?

He imagines the words that echoed within him—the names of trees, stars, and
        friends—sit around him under the sole porthole in his cellar
They walk the adjacent sidewalk that he strolls
binding with the dust or the air
resisting the authority of words on paper, or conspiring with new ink
From the lips of this window, words that he cannot confess descend upon him. Sorrowful,
he apologizes to them:
    I am not the master of nature   I cannot place my head in its hands
    He came like one launching a history   He found himself bobbing on an
ocean of secrets
      * The women came as ships; they had the bodies of water
    "They came. Each one greedy, calculating. Blood ran in water"
                  (Baladhiri, *Futuh al-Buldan*)
) * "The three conquests: conquest of expression, conquest of sweetness,
conquest of revelation." (Ibn Arabi)
) Do not enter the sea, unless the sails are women
        * Al-Ghota[2] is a tent and desire is the knot that ties its ropes
        * The sky, in an ant's mind, is also an ant
        * You do not need to be a wave to understand the sand

After the bath and the musk
      your limbs brighten and rise   You'll desire to stand at the gates of
        mystery

Tell your body then, as it follows its secret, to soak in the light of the door
of deliverance/genitalia—

> * No matter which of these two words you choose, you will not
> turn words into things
>
>) * Speak about what happened, not about what's to come. Wage
> wars, if you wish, but only between your lower and upper
> lips

He arrived
and when he spoke of planets, he preferred Venus. She used to meet him, lying on her
bed, and spoke to him only after she put out her candles
Prophecies, you are exempt from visiting him. His mind is taken by regions that you
would never go to or could return from

> * O train of ink, he has no stations on his papers
> * Let him sleep in the arm of this word: Love
> * He has yet to understand stone; he will not be able to write well
> on wings
> * Blood thinks, the body writes

As you exit the door of deliverance toward the door of peace, be assured that history is a
tunnel studded with lures of all kind

It is called

the door of the Honorable one, the door of safety. He was too powerful for those who tried to
conquer, he was guarded by trees that resembled bludgeons, swords, rifles. Water nymphs
also protected him, mermaids—the rivers Barada, Aqrabani, Daiyani. "His name was like a
gate unto itself, for peace and greetings. People came in droves to salute their caliphs." The
arch offered them a place in the shade that now shades new visitors for a new

salutation. Light itself is glittering, a mirror in which people find their faces as they enter
and leave. There are soldiers there, like angels that the eye can't see

> * Damascus, your seed is not in his hands, not in his steps, what
> good will your fields do him?
> * Wherever he finds a storage trunk he stops to awaken
> Wadah of Yemen,[3] and invites him on a leisurely stroll

Here is Jareer offering his life to the caliph in the annals of poetry . . . And I see Al-Akhtal
handing his friends, as the caliphate observes, his oldest secrets . . . And I hear al-Farazadaq
stuttering in the presence of a woman who neither praises nor condemns and who spoke
only of love. Drink from Dhil-Rimma's springs—look at him walking any distance that leads
to the horizon. The caliphs disappear; each one is shrinking to a hair, or a coin, or a sword[4]

> * My sky—not above my head, but under my shoulder: Peace to
> the great Imam
> * What wonders in this place that Ibn Taymiya[5] once called "my
> orchard"
> * The horizon distributes the chants of the minarets, while paradise
> is spread at the feet of Qassiyun[6]

Become a follower of Saturn, so to excel at revelation by the gate of Kissan, or to descend in
a basket, like St. Paul, dangling from the walls, escaping to Greece or whatever is behind the
sea. Like him, do not seek a door for itself, but for what hides behind it. You open it to see
what it discloses/encloses. Maybe you'll ask, is the body a door? And what is the body's door,
and where does it lead? And why is it not inhabited by anything unless it is called
ephemeral? Are the most beautiful places the ones that you place your body within, and that
reside in you when you cannot see them? Don't forget to imagine a door full of beauty open
wide to a door full of emptiness. And don't forget the iron circle with which you knock on
the door so that you may hear "yes!" It allows you to swim in the most beautiful lakes of
light or allows you to remain in your familiar darkness. Is life a door—real and symbolic?

Arches   lines that straighten, bow, spiral   circles and half

circles   squares, rectangles, pyramids, pentagons

octagons   shapes at the whims of calligraphy

* We met—we did not speak, we gesture
* Streets—rivers rubbing their banks against the music of history
* Jasmine sings in a low voice, walks the alleys barefoot
)* White blood on the moon's bed
) Don't place the basket of dust in the hand of the wind
) Misery comes kneaded by the hand of God, stamped with his
      seal, and happiness comes a refugee dressed in the clothes
      of wilting roses
* Each star has a drum, dawn is a broken flute
) Black angels swim in pools of silver
) Streets—fields of plants that feed on meat
) The sky woke up and began to distribute the morning papers

Reality approaches you lightly and sits you on the tips of its fingers: its stones have vocal cords, and wherever you turn, reality's face appears like a mirage kissing the earth. Its days are a soft soil on which the grass of history grows . . .

Is life here a kind of mail carried in the satchels of sand?

And what is that luxuriant effeminateness that knows how to bring beds together, and how to climb to the silhouettes of desires and their rustlings? He becomes happy and thinks he is sad. He is tasting pleasure and thinks he is in pain

Damascus, write again, your history on the fronds of the date palms, on the shoulders of camels. My road into you is a hard one, and I walk it barefoot

Al-Shaghoor Gate—

    Dust is a wild horse, no way to tame it. The roads are covered with the imprints of
    his feet

Al-Faradis Gate—

    Bury him in his blood, forget not to forget him

Al-Jabiya Gate—

    a whirlpool inside language's head—

        * How can Jasmine greet a body where only anemones grow?
        * What of these names?—
        they offer only balsams and there is nothing in their bodies but
            wounds
        * Dreams, lean your sadnesses on the windows of my eyelashes
        * Qassiyun, you who travel while standing still, do you know that
            the seasons have given everything else to others, but
            entrusted me with their steps?

Damascus,

your shadow wears my body, and your doors surround me. Your secrets fall into me:
Happiness only resides in cuffs and folds

Cloisters

    A.

A window-triangle, the light of nature's essence cascades from it, and gusts of air
        shaped like horses,—

                              (Al-Shaifia Cloister)

B.

Stairways made of thighs and heels. Henna and saffron awaiting a green shooting star,—

(Al-Qadiriya Cloister)

C.

Salt forgot its feet in the water. The shadow of the world is lead dipped in embers, no difference there between speaking and mud. If there is such a thing as misery, it must be happiness. Dust sits down to rest on this threshold. And hasn't gotten up yet

—Can a woman mate with a male jinn?

—There has been a lot of dispute on this matter

—But it is allowed to curl the hair, and braid it

—A woman in paradise is paired up with her last husband, and it's been
said to her first—

(Al-Taqwiah al-Hanbaliya Cloister)

D.

Time has soft weak hands, and eternity has a mouth that never stops yawning.
Horses come from all directions and sit among kneeling people. Trees of Damascene rise take off their underclothes. Ah, how pleasure is effortless and confusion abounds!

(Al-Mawlawia Cloister)

E.

Laurels of stars dangle from the ceiling. The earth ruffles like a pair of wings, the elements are the cells of dreams. Solitude is the ink of travel,—

(Al-Naqshabandia Cloister)

F.

Walk over the heads of flowers, mix with their blossoms. Your hands are violets and pollen dust is climbing your body. Here you'll learn how days have skins more tender than those of seeds,—

(Al-Rifa'iya Cloister)

G.

An angle holds a brush and draws the emptiness
How kind they are these sails that descend from the sky!
Here the lover enters the species of the wordless and becomes like basil,—

(Al-Baktashiya Cloister)

*Become like the rose and live silently:
If you have to speak, utter nothing but fragrance.
*Is writing a dried-up nectar in an abandoned hive
*Stone is a book that teaches tolerance

Talismans

"Seek a virgin whose time is ripe
undress her, ruffle up her hair
give her a rooster and tell her, rove with it all around the fields.
Your plants will be free of plagues
and the ryegrass will die off instantly."

"Take a goat's hoof, a gazelle's horn, and roots of the lily of the valley, grind them with
hazelnuts, burn the mixture as an incense around the house.
All snakes and pestilence will disappear."

"Take the heart of a large owl
wrap it in wolf skin
tie it around your arm.
You will be safe from thieves and all insects
and you will be respected among men."

"Make a copper statue of a locust
and in the hollow
place a locust and fill the space with wax.
Bury it.
All locusts will disperse and not a single one will remain in the place."

"Take some fennel flower seeds
some black alder leaves,
and shavings of ginger.
Mix them and add the mixture to food.
The spirit of love will fill those who eat it."

(from *al-Milaha fi 'Ilm al-Filaha*)[7]

Escapades

What does a wall, what does smoke do between two breasts?   What work does a
policeman do   what does a prison   placed between the liver and
the eye? Is the horizon here a pillar of salt?   Oh, this air that fills this
space with wrinkles!

What do you do with the words you unearth while crouching in clay that evokes
        Adam?   What do you do with cities whose shores are abysses?   What
        do you do with streets that are nothing but floods of tears?
        It's better that you give this dove a kerchief to wipe its eyes

A cancer devours the body of reality and in the wind there are leaves that had not
        fallen from trees, but from people.   There is no ash in the air, only in the
        lungs

There is no mud in nature, only in the nature of man.

                * He apologizes about meeting others, whispering: a female jinn is
                        staying at my home
                * The fingers are the body's blossoms
                * They believe in the planets, and they acquire science by its scent
                * Bodies that learn to bow before they learn to walk
                * His first wise discovery: People are hens whose teachers are
                        foxes
                * These lines are posted above his bed:
                        "God is a friend of the poor in dream,
                                and the rich in reality"

      * "The poor are granted stones to suckle until they die": the author of this
          statement is an ancient one still alive
      * He describes people:
          "A fertile tongue, and a barren heart"
          and himself "a healthy eye and a wilted body"
      * He used to say, "Man is not a body, but a number. Some of him is
          subtracted in each passing day"
      * He struggles, but like someone who wants to turn stone into
          sheep

I must take apart the body of the night, one piece at a time, to write a single step of
      Damascus.
To uncover her day, I must dress her in night, and what I write must be dictated by not
      knowing my way.
She is probably right: Writing is for the devils and these devils are her horrors.
Is this how time fortifies itself against her?
To her   to this edifice where Artemis once lived   I pledge these words.
But will she ever bend to Ishtar's beckoning?

Prophesy, O Blind One

2003

CONCERTO FOR THE ROAD TO DANTE'S CHURCH

1.

Why does the air need us, we who were born in the embrace of chains?

Take me, metallic dove, flying goddess, take me where my body intermingles with ether, and my feet melt in air. Indeed, at this moment, I prefer the face of a god to many human faces.

The airport—you are here merely as a name on a list. A digit among digits. You cannot exit the narrow corridor that will fly you away. You are truly left in the hands of chance. Chance, I say, to avoid "fate," a word I dislike. Perhaps in your seat, someone who is now dead had sat, or a child who dreams of being a pilot, a football player, or a woman who does not stop crying.

No steps, no traces. You create a friendship between silence and your lips. You are truly alone with yourself now. You fall into it, light and free. You test your silence and fragility. You have the power now to ask it, are you who you are?

An old man dragging a suitcase stops at an office, asks and inquires. Behind him stands a skeleton in the likeness of a man. I look at the old man mumbling. I sense what he is saying: Whoever searches for comfort here is like a man chasing a spider's shadow.

The airport—a mechanical spider web. Different threads of metal. What this web knows may make the birds long to have metal wings.

Indeed, what humans need now is wisdom, the untamable kind.

But no one can move like a defiant sage except if he tears the chain of innocence from the sky's neck, and only if he seats the heavens on the throne of pleasure as our ancestors in Babel and elsewhere had done.

It's better for me to place the book of delusions under my arm, and improvise in the name of the ink of travel.

Travelers—a long rope. I take my place, anxious about the rope. A child stares at me. He awaits his turn with his mother outside the rope. He can't remove his eyes from the book opened between my hands as if he is asking indignantly, is this rope a school, a library?

A child-dream.

Don't stop dreaming, dear piece of clay.

The last corridor to the airplane. A woman kisses her drooping lover on the lips whenever he takes a step. A rhythm that equates steps and kisses. Next to me on the plane a woman pours herself on her seat like a thin light. A crooked nose. She is weeping. I do not dare ask her the reason.

Perhaps her heart, like this era, is full of holes.

The plane lands—

Wave your lives like a hand, a greeting to travel.

Why does the air need us, we who were born in the embrace of chains?

Before landing,

I was, while reading the air that blows from the living, detecting news from the dead,

not those taken by nature's wisdom, but

those in whom the ember of war is embedded, and I

had no fear composing this bit of defiant wisdom:

> Making death beautiful is a crime,
>
> not like tyranny, but like murder.
>
> But, but, do not stop dreaming, dear piece of clay.

2.

Jerome Bloch, Alberto Caramella, a conversation on the road to Florence about everything except Dante. I toss my suitcase into my room. The day is hot as if it has just been taken out of the sun's kiln. Fawzi arrives from Milan.

—Let's go first to Dante's house and church.

The house-museum. Old tiles that have known Dante's steps and their rhythm, especially when he spied out Beatrice. Etchings, as if embossed on Damascene silk, decorate the broad gray tiles that cover the house and its inner staircase. Some of them are now drawn by the hand of time, and some, time claims, are drawn by the hand of love. In the first room, on the first floor, you are received by a copy of the death sentence issued in absentia on 15/March/1302.

"The sword first, as it is in the house of the Arabs," I whisper to Fawzi. He answers smiling, "But Dante managed to escape," and adds, "Look, these are samples of letters Dante wrote, metered and rhymed."

Three floors are used for his papers and for papers about him. Nothing. I prefer the interior staircase that connects the other floors, I prefer the windows and the wood. The third floor has a window.
Three pots of Damascene rose.
Everything remains except Dante.
Other things on display bear his traces in this house-museum, another death sentence on him, and another on his city, Florence.
Despair in the vision, but the labor and care are matchless.
(No prophet can retain dignity in his own land.
Or rather, no land is ever fit for a prophet).

Next to the house is Dante's church. He stole glances of Beatrice there, stored images of her in dreams to retrieve them in poetry.

Beatrice is buried in this church. We see her grave, and bid it peace as if we are recalling the Arabs' farewell at the beloved's abandoned abode and the dirges of our ancestral poets. Before our last look, a throng of women enter the church in the company of a few men.

Next to the house and church, a shabby, pallid, narrow street called Dante Alighieri.

3.

Here where Dante used to dream and where he waited for Beatrice, a single image holds me: A creature the size of the earth, his head is religion and his body is politics, or his head is politics and his body is religion and what connects them is commerce.

Also, I see aluminum chairs being taken from cafés and spread out onto the street, grouped lovingly in the grace of the cathedral that has taken the liver of Florence as the seat of its throne.

I see nothing around this cathedral except pairs of scissors with sky-colored blades. I hear nothing except voices rising from the throat of time, or from the test tubes of a science we have yet to know how to name. I see nothing on the walls of this cathedral, raised high in the name of the heavens, doubtlessly to imitate them, except angels in the shapes of cars and bicycles and dancing dolls dressed in pink jeans.

I imagine Florence as a rose bush torn to shreds, blossom by blossom, between the hammers of tourism and the anvil of globalization. Surely, if Dante were alive he would have accepted his death sentence, as Socrates did, not to see his birthplace arrested and executed each day.

I imagine branches searching for air among sun rays that fall like tar on the city's eyelashes. I imagine Beatrice sitting at Dante's doorstep weeping and trying to read Ovid's "The Art of Love."

I imagine I see the city's other son, Machiavelli, walking the thin hair of politics, in front of a church named after Dante, testing the hypocrisy of the human race and pretending to himself that he came to pray.

I imagine hearing space guffawing at the death sentences Dante's city issued against him.

And now, I have become more certain that the prehistory that resides in people's stomachs is the one that wrote and still writes the history of their heads.
In fact, since Cain, blood has been the first pleasure.
In the past, one myth fought another, and one idol fought another. Today, one divine revelation fights another, one sky fights another, all sycophancies for this tortured, wretched body, the earth.

How do we tell the sun
          that her rays today are threads woven to fashion our shrouds?
With what language do we tell her that
her rising is a wound and her setting is nothing but a grave?

Oh, Dante! Tonight I see Florence's moon. He does not stretch his arms as he used to in the bed of your days. And nothing rings from his feet on his way to his loved ones except the sound of chains. Now they break those bells of remembrance between his feet.
As if life is turning (as your friend Al-Ma'ari had claimed) into a woman beggar and we have no one to talk to except the dead, as if the sky has been emptied and filled with lead.

Dante, the roads to the purgatorio, paradiso, and inferno still pour with tears. There is no one in the processions of the gods except corpses. Do the gods hate life so much?
I ask you and I cry from the gorges of my inferno: How strange monotheism is! How wondrous her planets! Why did they banish us from that country whose gates to eternity were the idols of the unknown?!

Where does the ignorance of your "paradise" come from? Why did you fail to recognize Eros in its azure hue? Who told her the grave is the warmer home? Who taught her death is happiness that never dies?

I declare, Dante (as you admit me into your inferno)
that one bough from a single branch of the tree of life is more divine, more glorious than all the forests of death.

Florence, I wrote nothing about you. Pardon me, I promise to honor you another day.

CONCERTO FOR 11TH/SEPTEMBER/2001 B.C.

Rest your backs against the cedars of God
or surrender to the wheels of the machine.

He, the defiant one, will chart the lower layers of creation,
empowered with water that carries desire
in an essence half lead and half myth,
in the avalanche of limbs
where the elements are shot and matter is shattered.
Eleven September 2001 B.C.   11 September 2001 A.D.
the science of another rhythm to conjoin nature and algae,
throat and sword, wind and soul.

And to you, my people, you may applaud the blood gushing from the vein of goodness
and you may prostrate to the divinity of desire in the temples of evil
in the flood of metal geysers
in waterfalls of fire
in stars carpeted with ash.

Apollo, god, lover, beloved,
can you still distinguish between a face and a pair of buttocks?
And you banished and despised one, rejoice and celebrate.
Paradise is here, there, under your feet.

He, the defiant one, will chart the lower layers of creation,
and dive into them, into the deepest depths.
He writes another history for voice, alphabet, and word.
To his right is a dromedary like Imruulqais's
on his left a spaceship.
(ص): a desert that never stops screaming
(ع): the work of the wind in the belly of sand
(ﻫ): the dream of a body that saw everything while still in the womb
(غ): the stars sang
(ي): the warrior king said:
Do not believe everything, wind. I ask nothing
of you except obedience,
and you, sky, where were you? Why were you slow to respond
when I invited you?

(ن): a sobbing in the throat of history—
Averros, Decartes, Hegel,
where are your brains now? In Tiberias? On the Hudson?
Or between them in a red rocket ship?

The present is a slaughterhouse
and civilization a nuclear inferno.

And what do you say about human beings, each of whom lives inside a ball of ice and has
        only one dream:
Where to stroll on the surface of Mercury?
And say: who colonizes the imagination of the West?
How can the hand of virtue grasp Moses' staff

and explode the fury of war?
And how did a thousand and one nights become a thousand and one armies?
And say, who had turned divinity into a form of entertainment?
My certainty resides
in the house of a spider.
And what is this crumbling among the ruins of orbits,
not a planet
and not a machine to conquer planets,
it is the poetry of matter.

Oh how now more than ever my senses need to read the holy books
with the eye of poetry.
Buddha will be happy.
Buddha reads with his body and loves poetry.

The lower layers of creation   *Kaf* ك   *Nuun* ن(Be)
Coincidence is the creature's home
not the end of words
not the seal of knowledge.

The lower layers of creation   *Ta* ت   *Siin* س
Camouflage your innards, technology. What are you inflicting now
on the body of the universe?
No matter how deep you delve, you will never reach the heart's unknown.
And how miserable you are, gift of art—
one brush breaking another,
one ink murdering another ink.

The lower layers of creation   *Qaf* ق   Lam   ل   (Say)

غ   Guantanamo

a prison administered by capitalism on a communist island

a space flooded with alphabets like the clay

of which Adam was made—("the earth is a whore," you said. But

is she not the mother of all the angels?)

ش   د   Human, animal shapes of all sorts are slaughtered and spread raw on the
          tables of time.

Blood spilled as if it is seeping from the gardens of God.

م   The enslaver/the enslaved   an adulteration or mollification of the
          dualism of master/slave.

س   ش   Sanctifying death   Virtue that is
          evil   Evil that is virtue.

And thought that is merely wash water.

In the beginning was crime

("What do they want

those who do not want peace or justice,

and do not want terrorism?")

Saint-Just, for example.

ه   (Is there anything human in a human being?)

ث   No revenge without justice: thus spake Aeschylus.

Revenge first, this is how New York speaks.

You have done well, Jim Morrison,[1] speaking of an American night.

Imruulqais, al-Mutannabi, Al-Ma'ari—

Say: who can now speak well of his planet . . . this Arab night?

Ah, how tired the earth must be!
Truly,
from the struggle between   ن   ي   and   د   (fuck)
the world's tragedy began.

2.

 م   a procession launches the birth of planets, dragged by a soldier star.
Legs led by blind men   where we read
the history of humanity
in a new translation
etched on the page of memory
with a plastic chisel.

And in the forest of uranium mushrooms
we build an oven that offers us bacterial bread.

I wish I knew how to tie the flag to the strings of dream.
I would have entered the bed of an oyster or mated with a tree.

Open my chest wide. Where are your arms, jasmine tree?
And you migrant bird, is it better to be hunted
in the land of your migration than to be choked in your parents' bed?

Do not forget to kiss for me the first branch that
received your wings   and I will kiss in your name
the air, for no reason, except to test the chain that clamps
my lips.

3.

ح   The most beautiful thing that distinguishes the body of the sea is that it is captive
to the recklessness
of waves.   When will we place nature's wedding ring
on the finger of God?
I ask and I know:
Ignorance, here-there, the key to knowledge.
Will I be mistaken if I said to necessity, bring your fruits. And to chance, pluck them?
Will I be mistaken if I said, culture has become a tunnel where we learn
how to obliterate life and exterminate mankind?
We erase color and replace it with mud.   We imprison
the alphabet of the tongue and release the alphabet of the foot.   We slay
knowledge on a slope of a history dripping with blood.
Will I be mistaken if I say: the road to tomorrow is an open wound?
I will clarify all this in a letter that I will address to the sun.
Life, I do not want to complain about you, or complain to you.
I only want to say this: I am still in love with you.

Gilgamesh on that night of September 2001 B.C.
found the herb that defeats death. He did not know
how to pluck it or cut it. Tiresius' prophecies later
filled Homer's eyes with a darkness that slides
down the thighs of the gods on Mount Olympus while one of Ulysses' flies scratched
the skin of night, night
that walked on one leg   while Penelope
woke up screaming: What a world!

Flies in the day,

mosquitoes at night.

And I said to alembics as they conversed with a microscope,

or as they dripped into semiotic test tubes

where love had the shape of an ovum and poetry

traveled at the speed of light,   I said,

How weak a house must be

when its wisdom is

dictated by the ink of New York.

4.

A Sumerian God listened to me wetting his feet with water

that unites the Tigris and the Euphrates.

God, you who are also a friend, did you once whisper

to your wife, "It is difficult even for God

to be himself in this world"?

Suddenly,

a troop of angels fell upon us and began to stone language.

And because words are fire, silence is the beginning of hell.

I had woven a dress for New York with the threads of this language.

I stayed up many a night there

among the echoes of un-emaciated heifers[2]

surrounded by dancing nuclear debris, and I saw

creatures made of cardboard chanting songs

written by hydrogen frogs.

5.

You can, poet, poke your nose in everything,
and shove what concerns you into the nose of your era.
You can set up camp on the forehead of the sun, and say
to your armies of images and your powers of visualization to stand guard at night
protecting the earth.

You can declare: Tragedy is the root of sky.
And you can point out: Stone, even in Baghdad, is about to drip out of shame.
It is not improbable that by now
the Tigris is wearing a long gray beard and leaning on a staff
and the Euphrates is trembling in terror
from an attack prepared by the silt of history.
You may not be surprised by this headache that quakes the universe. You may
hear a phone commanding you not to fear, and the most song-filled
of the Arab capitals will dance: Divination has proven
that the whole world is at its disposal.

6.

I was in my wretched room in Paris, trying to have my country sit
on my knee,
              not to heal it as Rimbaud did with beauty,
but to catch the scent of autumn that hides shyly within her,
and so that I may compare it with the poet's face, and possibly declare
new rights for mankind that I still hesitate to announce.

A knock on the door.
No weapons here. Nothing except books.
Huh, who said letters do not bear arms?

Reality tears at Marx's argument, and here the class struggle is a lost
cloud, and imagination whispers to us, "I doubt we are
the end of the vegetable horizon. I suspect we are stone tossed into water
to punish the devils of dust."

But I have been learning, even before 11 September 2001 B.C., how to color my ink with
resistance, how to place my catch of prophecies midair inside a quiver carried by a lovesick
dove. I've always known that bombs do not know enough to envy the planets.
Light befriended everything, and the gods were the skin of the world.
O how words in their old age long for the childhood of the alphabet!
Earth, allow the moon to circle his arm around your waist.
Until that time, the world will sit weeping, wiping its tears
with the bodies of the dead.

7.
How tired the earth is!
—Screams from a green audience.
—Have no fear, my country. This is the way you are. I will take you to the cedar at the end of
time.

8.
"Everything is finished," says a witness who is dying.
It is the era of humans who are not born
until their old age.

Truth is dreadful, a creature born dead.

Child inside of me, repeat to me your love for beautiful ruins. Assure me again that to
read is to write the future.

This is how out of destruction and foolishness

I raise my body to you, love.

Peace to you, ether that only the eyes of a lover can see.

And you, poetry,

will you continue your gifts, taking us to coincidences,

states where we see again people, creations, things, impulses,

abundance, diversity, uniqueness,

the wakefulness of nature and the insomnia of matter?

Will you take us where we can declaim:

No star exists that your imagination has not penetrated,

no sky exists that has not pronounced your name?

Will you take us to our same earth, the one that spins

on our wounds, where we can scream:

Rosy explosion in the volcanoes of our lives

when will you put a limit to the despair of this earth?

9.

In fog shifting between orange and the color of coffee,

I try to probe this rising century,

but I cannot detect a gravitational pull

even though I had transferred the whole matter to Mercury

and have thrown my arms waving to Mars and his guests and neighbors.

My path is obscured by smoke and fire

and in all directions I see nothing except a mysterious boiling gushing.
How can I caution of what's to come,
when caution itself is terror?

10.
Lean on the cedar of god
or surrender to the wheels of the machine.
He, the defiant one, will become a refugee
searching for the liver of the world.

Paths split by the blood of capitals—Jerusalem and cities
that build their thrones on the body's joints—
where the dead live in books and in windows,
where the living lie in corridors of emptiness,
he will become a refugee, he who grew on the same earth where Christ
was born
between a tree about to be torn out
and a lamb about to be led to slaughter.

And who is he, who faces
four billion
and fifty six million
turns of the earth
around a sun
preparing for its twenty-sixth revolution
in the circumference of the galaxy?
No,
he wishes only to brighten his steps.

Love, will you not teach him again
how to mingle with other creatures,
how to pluck the lyre of the universe?

11.
Well,
what will she wear tonight,
this poor lover, the earth,
Ishtar's linen or New York's silk?

And you, lover,
with which sky
are you going to dance?

CONCERTO FOR THE VEILED CHRIST

1.

I never saw roads fly as I saw them in Turin, Monday, 18/2/2002. I wanted to reach the airport, fearing I would get lost, or miss the plane as happens to me often.

At the same time I needed to see the statue of "the Veiled Christ" by Sammartino. How I envy him his poetic technology that reflects the pains of Christ, contentedly, as no technology had ever shown them before. A wave in the shape of a statue; the water is a crumbled, wrinkled kerchief wrapping a body in pain where the wrinkles say: All of pain is embodied in this body.

I wanted to drink coffee again at Café Intra Moenia on Bellini Square, and to see the Church of San Domenico and its piazza, and the Nile church ("the terrifying place," a plaque on its entrance says in embossed Latin), and the statue of the Nile erected to salute the merchants of Alexandria who built Naples.

But the road was flying   under a sun that began to loosen its long braids   on balconies that stretched their rose-filled hands to the horizon. The colors in the opulent alleyways began to shift to better remember old faces, Greek and Roman, and the echo of steps . . . (Boccaccio, Petrarch, Thomas Aquinas, Giotto, Sammartino) . . . steps on the same tile that my feet have loved (everything has changed except the tile).

I recalled Al-Ma'ari and "the dust of creation" and I said, "perhaps I should step lightly as I walked."

Do you think the dust that covers the gray tiles on the church's threshold comes from Aquinas's body or Giotto's? Is the hand of that dust now touching my shoulder? And the air of this era, from which dust is it coming?

Francesca tried to catch signs of that era still waving at us.   Francesco tried to record rhythms for a poetry and music composition we were writing together while we all waited for Guinaro.

But the roads were flying, and history hung suspended above us not knowing where to place his feet on earth amidst the throng that reminded me of Antioch and Beirut.

My eyes asked me, how can exile still ring in someone's steps while exiting a hall at the University of Turin   after he had spoken of "the other" and where he said, "There is nothing in the self except the other?"

Thank you Naples for your sun that loves to lean on my shoulder   for your breakers that mirror themselves in my memory crashing against my limbs.   Do you still need an explanation, you, who refuses to read?

Francesca, Francesco, Guinaro, have you said "meet again"?

Friendship again   but the roads are flying.   How can coming together be like a tree soaring through a cosmos made of cement? How to translate the scent of roses, beautiful one, who asks about translation?

Translation can grow old   but poetry is ageless.

Will Naples remain the sweet air that blows between Beirut and Alexandria? And what is this time   as if carrying its harrowing axe about to strike the face of the east, or as if Rome is no longer where Rome used to be?

Francesca to the train   Francesco to the airport in a little while.

Cars leaping one after the other   red is green.
No astrologer has said this   but eternity is the light of a candle whose rays break at the corners of meaning.

Did I say the coffee was not good?   Goodbye Francesco, the roads are flying.
         I enter the gate that will lead me to the plane.

I discover that I did not check my luggage, and did not get a boarding pass.   Here's Alitalia, here's Lufthansa.   Roads of the world, guide me!

At seventy, I am still a child. God, what are you doing to me?   What am I doing to myself?   The older I get the more I feel I am an inexperienced child   an ignorant child   especially in travel.   I need someone to take me by the hand when I travel.   My steps become confused   my eyes befuddled.   I feel I should always ask someone to tell me where and how   as if I'm inhabited by a fear of loss   of getting on an airplane that is not going where I want to go   or a train taking me to where I do not intend to go.   A nail clipper   paper scissors the size of a finger.   "These will not fly with you to Munich,"   said the Italian police woman.   How did she see in my face a hostage taker's when I've always been a hostage?   "Very well, you can have them then."

2.

In the gate   I sat to think about what I was and what is happening to me.   I
was almost tired from the roads that fly inside me.

This is how I began to write what you are reading now, reader.

The roads are still flying   but around the statue of "The Veiled Christ"
          in Cappella Sansevero—
No, the veil will not unveil itself from its meaning—
Can a single human being be born out of two wombs?

Oh, there isn't a single star in this drink   and the moon that drowned in this glass
has been pressed and choked until it became a crescent,   almost.   Why
can't I see the abyss as a green house sometimes?   Will I wait long in Munich?
          And what will I do in Berlin this evening   and where does this desire come
from, to mix letters whose words are not easily read?   Why do I feel that order is only
a way of choking words?   The plane hasn't arrived in Munich.   I feel I have
not left Naples, that I am still mixed with it.   Hybridity or mongrelization?
          At any rate, the future will be either bastardly or murderous.

As if I have not left Naples, I who let her be trampled by roads that were flying.

You read your poetry in   Galassia Gutenberg.   You are surprised that you
have an audience in translation greater and better than in your original language.   Is
this the beginning of mongrelization?   Pardon me, mother tongue to whom only the
miseries of your children cling.

Francesco, how were you able to harmonize the Arabic rhythms with your Italian cadences
    between the word that slides from the mouth of the sky to the one rising from the
mouth of the earth?   Is this how the Naples roads, flying among a thicket of sparrow
wings, were rescued by a citizen poet?   Or flying out of the chests of Arab
immigrants who spit blood avoiding or escaping that other blood their nations spit?

"I work here. I don't know when I will return," said a physician.

"I write poetry in the language of the country that sheltered me," said a young man who
looked old.

"I will never return to my country," said a young woman, almost crying.
Indeed, how miserable it is to be an Arab today.
Tell me, you dark, exiled, and banished one, in what language does the dawn of Naples
whisper to you?   And you who never fail to wake each day   to
embrace her like a child who has just awakened from sleep   each day   tell
me.

And the roads were flying around the statue of the Veiled Christ.

With a nail, Christ is veiled   with a plank of wood   with a ceiling of cloud

with the dome of a chemical planet   with a voice that crosses continents

with the face of a worker not working   with corners leaking blood   with
peripheries and ruins.

Oh, where does this creature come from   from each word uttered by his mouth a
sword comes out striking splitting throats?   An angel at times   a human at
others.

I know that the light sometimes changes into a mask worn by fingernails.
Cup, with whom will you share your bread?
The body is stubborn and the head has other bread.
Prayer, I invite you to the last supper.

3.

The plane swims.   I swim with it over mountains of cloud.   It has begun to
land.   I now imagine the flying roads of Naples also landing.   What shall I
call their flying?   You are only passing, cloud that looks like a gazelle.
          Nothing remains of a cloud, not even the word "remain."   Landing.
          Earth and space on this trip are a single carpet.   I am falling asleep. I slept
little last night after I read an article that said, "sleep little to live long."   The plane
has landed.   I had never known the irksome face of childhood before this trip.
          Another attribute to be added to roads that fly over the Mediterranean.

Who put those rocks on the heads of his waves?

The atom's inquisition?   The blood of wars?   And this fire that leaps from
tree to tree in his blessed forests   and these graves that open their depths to children
and their mothers.   And this everpresent illness wearing a disappearance cloak.

Take my body, Mediterranean Sea.   Place it beside Cadmus and Dante.
          Repeat after them,   Beauty is the earth's alphabet and the alphabet is the
femininity of the universe.

I think, that I, this planet of dirt,
can no longer see except with my severed limbs.

I think I am preparing to enter through the window of myth.

The sun is rising over the Levant stumbling in her old trousers. Tremble all you want now, branches of Damascene rose, celebrating the wind.

I IMAGINE A POET

A salute to Jacques Berque[3]

I imagine a poet
in Beirut, sister to Anatolia, friend of Athens,
a poet who stands with his friend Jacques Berque at the gate of the sea
leaning on his cane.
I imagine his voice as the sound of a tambourine,
that the tambourine is broken in his throat,
that his throat is a fire named God.

I imagine a poet
into whose innards history pours
drenching his words and pooling at his feet,
a poet who rains blood that some hoist as a banner made of sky.

Goddess of doubt, you who were born in the lap of our mother the sea,
why do you not announce this poet and his friend?
Say what you do not see,
what turns time on its back,
what holds the wind standing on tiptoe,
what pours the ashes of silence on the flames of speech
improvised by the world's prose.
Announce also the inflamed eyelashes
the severed hands
the withered days

and whether the lantern is a throat or a head
and how we can distinguish today between an insect and a flower.
And say is there a means now
to colonize the clouds?
And say
how this Mediterranean still needs
to reemerge from the childhood of the alphabet.

Alphabet, how brave they are these cicadas that inhabit your harvest,
how ferocious these angels that lie in the beds of your forgetfulness!
René Char
where is the storm then,
and why is poetry still an ally of the waves
and why has the sky left nothing of our history
except statues whose genitals have been cut off?

The poet leaning on his cane
standing at the gate of the sea, with his friend
Jacques Berque
whispers to his friend, or perhaps to the waves:
"If there is a sky, it is migration."

And his friends replies, also whispering,
"No
the miracle is not above;
it's the soil sleeping among the underclothes of the grass."

What time is it now? I don't know
except that the spidery arms of the clock spin. Two or three flies circle and buzz above.
Poet, write a poem, and describe the scene
adding the wall upon which you were hung   and the curtain
half torn under the lamp   and the black window.
Do not forget to allude to modernity   so that you may be counted
among the pioneers, but before that, don't forget to describe the scene,
the old shoe resting alone   under the clock as if
waiting for its owner's return, and beware of the big issues: Poetry
must capture—not the things—but their crumbs.
And let your words rise to their covenant.

Owah!
The moon has fallen sad asleep
on his chair covered with clouds.
And the poet leaning on his cane accompanied
by his friend Jacques Berque
counted the moths that drowned in the clamor of the flame
on that night,
the flame of candles lit by children
who spend their nights standing in foam
hunting the waves.

An evening in Beirut,
lost and pining like a beggar soliciting in the vastness of space
brought down to his knees
resting his cheek on Ulysses' cheek.
Do we think we are still alive by the shore of the Mediterranean,

have we become herders of the stars?
A rose carries the whole of night in her sleeves,
leans on Beirut's chest,
and gives her waist to the air's forearm
while life embraces her hatchlings
placing her feet on the staircase of the future.

Is this really the world?
Shall I grieve? Shall I hope?
I prefer to sing.

Beginnings of the Body, Ends of the Sea

2003

The rose leaves its flowerbed
                    to meet her
The sun is naked
in autumn, nothing except a thread of cloud around her waist

This is how love arrives
in the village where I was born

Your mouth's light, no redness
can match its horizons

Your mouth, the light and shadow
of a rose

In her name
I do not wish to exist so to exist

I make my lights blaze
and track my time
in her embrace

and I sing to us and sing to her
in her name—

Friend of my capture, her luminous body, teach me how to sing again

I wake and ask dawn about you: Have you woken?

I saw your face sketched around the house
on every branch   I carried dawn on my shoulder:
            She arrives,
or is it the dream tempting me?
                        I asked the dew
on the branches, I asked the sun, have they read
        your footsteps? Where did you touch the door?
        How did they walk alongside you, the roses and the trees?

I am about to break my days and split in two:
my blood there, my body here—sheets of paper
dragged into the ruined world by sparks

                    ❁

I imagine my love

    breathing with the lungs of all things

    and it reaches me

    as poetry

    of roses or dust

    speaks softly to everything

    and whispers its news to the universe

    the way the wind and sun do

    when they split nature's breast

    or pour the ink of day

    on the earth's book

Our night is quiet
      Over here flowers bowing
      over there something resembling a stutter
      no trembling, no artifice

Our night sighs in our lungs
      and the windows shut their eyelids

—Are you reading?
—Make us some tea   —A light
seeps from our bodies to our bodies
and changes the face of the place

Every day we reach toward our bodies—
      we turn over our days
      in their books

      One fruit
      but the picking is a country
      that has no borders

❁

When we meet   wherever our steps take us   in cities
        or fields   let silence
        enter its wound-speech

Do you want my love to have a face that lights the sky? Then let
        your eyes become a house for my face   Take me—talk
I cannot feel the rhythm of my body in your hands and eyes
        unless you speak

❁

Love, give him, another body

    because where no travel is possible
    he wanted to take the earth by the throat
    and to ascend, journeying
    the midday heat of its passions

    And now in his earth night has buried
    his first murdered body

So yes, give him another body, O love

Every day
there is a dialogue between my face and its mirror
No, not to read love
and not to read the changes in my features
or the lightness of death in my gaze, but
to teach my love
how to ask the mirror: Why do I not sense
the night-nature of existence, the essence of its unknowns and mine?
Why do I not sense my life
except when I look into my face?

Moon—how kind the moon is
       when it comes and draws water from her pool
       then says goodbye, fleeing
how kind, the bed, the mattress, the covers
       where our
       limbs used to entangle
       in a long embrace as we begged the angel of wakefulness
       to walk his bridge
       but to slow his pace

How kind the planets were—they sang
       whenever evening brought us together
       and undressed our news

❖

How can I call what is between us a past?

"What is between us is not a story
not a human apple or a jinn's
not a sign of a season
or a place
not anything that could be historicized"   This is
what the vicissitudes inside us say

How can I say then that our love
has been taken by the wrinkled hands of time

❁

"Each love is a misery"—
      or as some of its mad men have said
            "Happiness is an illusion in love"

I do not love so to take something—
My love is not a mask or a flag
The way a spring gushes
the way the sun gleams
      I love: a flood   no purpose

My love is not illusion
My love is not misery

❀

Maybe
there is no love on earth
except the one we imagine
we will win   some day

Don't stop
Go on with the dance, dear love, dear poetry

even if it were death

I imagine I am the sound of singing
rolling in waves among the bending reeds
I mix with light in the sun's chamber
       in the tents of the trees
I hide
among springs sometimes
and sometimes I descend the slope
of depths I cannot see

Ah love—a spring
falling aslant from the heights of fatigue

344

From nothing
where meaning
wanders in the wilds
love comes, and remains strange
wider than we had pictured, and higher

Is there refuge among these embers burning?

❀

I will not sing my song—
        No song if it is not burdened
with the bitterness of love
and what the wind's folly leaves suspended
                in the air

No song
unless its equivalent
emerges from the edge of weeping

❁

Ah, no

> I don't want my eyes to swim in any space
> other than his eyes   No
> I don't want my love and its possession to become clearer
> I don't want belonging, or lineage, or identity

I want us to become a language
for euphoria, an alphabet of limbs

❁

Let's return
to streets we used to wander in
where we saw the world settle
in the lakes of our breathing and time come and go
through broken windows

We walked on our ruins, into the mirrors of our follies
into the dictionaries of dead paper
and our steps left no trace

Let's walk again
in the gardens of our high days

I don't love you except for that I hated you once—
one, multitudinous in his body

Ah, how deep love is in its hatred
Ah, how deep hatred is in its love

❁

I measured myself to the woman I imagined
I went out seeking her but found
nothing bearing a trace of her—
no bridge
between my body and my dream

This is how I began to live in what I imagined—
how delusion and I became friends

I will visit the place that was summer for us
after we traveled
between Ulysses' shores, through the night of Delphi
 and the sun of Hedra
and I will walk the way I used to walk
lost among trees
I will remind his flowers and herbs
of the fragrance of our meeting

They will surely ask about you: What became of you?
 Where are you? Which way do you face now?
 But

what am I saying?
when seasons have erased other seasons

Bitter insomnia comes to light its candles

Should I return my love's letters to their ink?
Should I tear these pictures?

I read my body now
and I fill the candle of this long night with sadness

I check my house at night   I turn on lights
but they do not light up   Windows? I begin to open
the windows but they bring no light / Maybe I'll find some
light through the door, I say
and begin to plead with it
but it does not illuminate / Darkness here is like a wound
that even as it heals continues bleeding—
Love says to me

      Oh Love, how can light shine
      when sky betrays sky

I began to love that bed covered with our day
On its breast we flung our visions, sighs, and secrets
Now I almost see it staring at me, asking about us—
Our news?
Drowning among corridors, I lean on that bed
        and declare my love to that screaming
        that explodes in its silences

Me sleeping? No sleep, only wakefulness that pains me
and infatuations too—the echo of an era: What brings it back?
House? Some pictures here—The key to a caravan
of love letters   This is a room whose colors
have dimmed and the ash
of our days is spread all over it   Here, books
covered with dust   A horizon—at play
in the wind, no lightning in it, no rain—
What are these pictures doing here?

Sleep? No sleep   Only wakefulness that pains me
The moaning of our forests   The dead our fruit

Orpheus—I can swear that I see him—
    the women tearing him apart and the wind
    running with his limbs
    As if touching his cheeks, I ask him:
    Which of them cut off his head?
    And I am surprised
    poetry did not find him
    love could not find him

Ocean whose waves intertwine
among the chords of his guitar
console us—tell us

Is it true that you saw Euridice among them?

I learn—I insert my eye among your eyes' alphabet
until I see in a moment
how your eyes write my eye
how our limbs fall
in the trap of life
how our dreams dissolve
in the lakes of our motionless days

Time is not a bed, the earth is not sleep
the trees of love are leafless
and the place that love desired is bare

Could it be that night awakened his dreams
        and they're now running down the sun's streets? I suspect
that these suns yawning
        in love's orbit
        are nothing to the earth but wounds

I will sing to this place
with the ruins of the lover who came before me
This creation is nothing but a clearing for a song

Dusk takes time by the throat
      and dangles it in a hole
      where my love's prophecies writhe
      half-choked

The suns that life still searches for
      hide in a child's face
      who emerges from the femininity of his dreams

❁

What did we lose, what was lost in us?
To whom do these distances belong that separated us
and that now bind us?

Are we still one
or have we both broken into pieces? How gentle this dust is—
Its body now, and mine, at this very minute
are one and the same

I vow that you are the root—I tried to read
      what remained of it, to pronounce the silence:
      No sound   How did this muteness
      find us, this muteness
      that is a language in itself? My face
      and your face, this evening, an ocean
      for a wound's vessel—
      The face of its pilot is cold
      No place on it for "no" or "yes"

❀

After all this roving that has filled the world
        after the years have worn out my body
I sing to us, to our childhoods

I can't believe that I have become old, I walk, a stranger
No consolation needed, I do not complain—My love and death
        are in one orbit   but I still wish to tempt
        those that come after me
to light the darkness of eternity
with the body's glow

❀

Life took us to it, tossed us
        in the nets of its storms and gave its breast
        to the windows of our days

When I ask myself: What did we take? and I see   I see nothing
        in the windows except nets

Could we have deluded ourselves
        like our ancestors
        that we're out of the nets? Are we
        like our ancestors
        who still love the life that loved its chains?

❀

Every time you say, "These are my paths etched on you," languages
that arose from unknown regions of my youth begin to grow
suspicious   From where has my conscience gained
this bitter travel into doubt?

Imagined vessel sailing
the darkness of my love's
tidal waves,
take me to you, help me
hold on to my self

A barrier between us—
      a barrier of blood
      a barrier of height

          from barren winds
          and lightless planets

A barrier that writes death and love in one vernacular
a barrier of powerless desire

❀

A room betrayed by sleep   No dream   And night is a grave
            opening, and the door is a cane of light
            and the chairs—no joy
                    A phantom of sand
                    obscures all their colors

A room—
            nothing in it except death reading its walls

❀

Will it console you that the clouds come and go in seconds
that other clouds come after them?
Will it console you that graves are houses
where people
become equals among their walls?
Will it console you that our seeing

only captures what the clouds draw? My consolation
is that the place from where I came
still whispers its secrets
to me, and that the time to which I belong
still renews its colors
turning over its leaves
in the book of trees

Sunset—

      Has the hour of not returning to the sunrise of love
          come?

A room—and the minarets in every direction
      are chattering within the shade of its walls
      He remembers   A death
          on the pillows under the cover
          turning its pages   Dust
          and scrolls of dreams

and dictionaries for dead reality   Love—dusk

Ah, how far the East is from love, from its inheriting sun!
Ah, how beautiful tragedy is!

Here's her house—
        all its doors are wounds
        the windows are shrouded
        with curtains   whose edges
            are fringed with strange flowers
            without coronets

In the darkness the curtains have imposed
            a night of abandonment and despair
            Its bleeding specters
            settle in the abyss of my stormy depths

❀

Have I told you the wound? But   (in between there was a lot
unsaid) We entered   our house (what we called our house)
Our window was pronouncing our love   Have I told you the wound?
(Were you listening?)   A wound   our night is still
not free from its echo   from its chain

Its chain   is what we made ourselves believe
was our love

What is he saying?

          Those who loved him have died

          Those whom he loved killed him

Springs of his love

if anyone inquires about him, embrace him, and say:

"He walked past here

he did not say his name

and he did not stop"

Printer of the Planets' Books

2008

YOU ARE IN THE VILLAGE THEN

1.

When he leaves home carrying his axe, he is certain that the sun is waiting for him in the shade of an olive tree, or a willow, and that the moon that crosses the sky tonight over his house will take the road closest to his steps. It is not important to him where the wind goes.

2.

The blueness of the sky, the redness of fruit, the greenness of leaves: These are the colors that his hands spread on the page of day.

He is an artist who cares about his hands' work, not what the hands of art achieve, but the things inside things, and not as they appear, but how he describes them. And because he knows how to listen to things and how to speak to them, he lives on the margin of what people perceive. He believes that "the order that imprisons motion and interrupts the feasts of the imagination will only lead to collapse."

And it collapses without theatrics or noise. He knows "that a bullet now replaces his plough," but he also knows, with growing certainty, that "his plough will go further and that it will reach deeper than any bullet can."

3.

When you see this farmer carrying his plough, you sense then that he is competing with it as if in a war. It proceeds ahead of him toward the weeds and thorns and he remains barefoot following behind. The sound of the plough, as it tears at the thorns and soil, joins you, penetrates you, and it's lovely to hear it become loud like a trumpet with a deep raspy blow filling the sky.

4.

You are in the countryside then. It does not matter where you walk now, near the river or at the foot of a mountain, or a village lost among the rocks, where mud houses mix with cement cellars in a folkloric symphony that combines the tenth and the twentieth centuries. Let your eyes swim in all that's around them, forget the café and the street. Surrender like a leaf flying in the air, like the fuzz coating the branches, like pollen dust. Become a child. Only then will invisible creatures come toward you. Solitude filled with a treasure of hidden murmurs. Absence that instantly becomes a presence. Each tree is a person, each stone a sign.

There are herds of small animals that shine like distant stars, among grasses and plants. And there are stones that have heads and arms and that may walk behind you at night. There are small streams flitting among small trees that become beautiful maidens who appear to tired people heading to their houses before dawn, during the first hours of enchantment.

5.

The village is not a poet, as much as it is a painter. There is a remarkable ease to its touch as it draws the same picture every single day maintaining the same beauty. It is repetition that does not repeat the same motion, something like the waves of the sea, or like the desert renewed endlessly in sand, its only dress.

There is no uniqueness to this touch as if it comes from an absolute neutrality forever positioned at degree zero.

6.

You are in the village then?

I remember now what I almost forgot. To contradict the light in the village, one will end up choosing solitude, sitting on the other side of the mountain, or the square, or among the barefoot children and black goats.

And I remember now that we used to gaze at the stream covered with green grasses, hardly able to determine its course. We thought it was in pain, and moaning.

And I now know why we felt dried up in the memory of the stream.

And in the days now inscribed in the dust of the road leading to the stream, I also read what we knew and did not know how to write:

Peace to the sun that always went ahead of us, without ever moving.

WAKEFULNESS

In the village, I always wake before the sun so that I can take a better look at the first steps that the morning draws on the stairway of space. Also to better see the wakefulness of the other shapes on the theater that surrounds me. They are shapes that change according to the changes of light and shadow. For each tree, for each plant, for each stone there is a wardrobe full of clothes to wear and take off. This all depends on the place—a tailor with beautiful hands, a magical face, one cheek in the shade and one in light.

It is a moment that makes me feel that the movement of things is what writes the world with an ink that is nothing less than the blood of time.

As wakefulness continues, and seeing continues, a feeling fills me that on this stage appearance is the eternal presence, and that meaning is the eternal victor.

RAG

I walk—nothing to hold on to but hands
        that I barely see.
The leaves of time fly about as I ask,
why can I never finish reading them?

At the doorstep of the café, at the beginning of the street, poetry came
and went in the shape of a seer
on a day that was like a rag wet with muddy water.

MUSIC

Nothing, nothing—a light wind plays the trees' guitars.
Nothing, nothing.
Emptiness. No way for words to fill it.

And I dream, dream
and the dream is nothing but reality in its infancy.
So ask yourself then, don't ask me—
there is no blockade against the horizon except in your mind.
But, it is almost certain
that a poem rises magically like a house dangling from the sky.

In this house an immigrant lives and his name is meaning.

MOTION

I travel outside my body, and inside me there are continents
that I do not know. My body
is in eternal motion outside itself.
I don't ask: From where? Or where were you? I ask, where do I go?
The sand looks at me and turns me into sand,
and the water looks at me and brothers me.

Truly, there is nothing to dusk but memory.

WAR

War—time walks on, leaning on a cane made from the bones of the dead.
Lead holds its feasts on rugs woven by human eyelids.
Skulls pour blood, skulls get drunk and hallucinate.

War—chains proceed in a festival of broken necks.
History is feet, the days are shoes.

War—heads are flung in a dusty field without a goalkeeper or goal. In ash draped on the
streets, in streets dressed in their severed limbs. Not even the sun can illuminate this body
that bleeds darkness. And the sun almost says to its light:
Dazzle my eyes so that I do not see.

War—dawn rusts in an alembic filled with lead, in an air that rots on a horizon of black
magic, in blood that walks the book of dust, in dust that wears human faces.

War—minds collapse, ideas are rags fluttering their flags. Who can say where mankind lives
now? Who can confirm that this is our mother earth? In every moment, one more of love's
offspring dies. The rose forgets to release its fragrance. War-resurrection writes. Death reads,
the corpses are ink.

War—Will we make paper out of death on which to write our days? Have we begun to
understand the silence of stone, the intelligence of crows, the owl's wisdom?

War—the heifer of damnation is adorned with the knives of piety, as if life were a mistake corrected only with murder.

FACE

The other face/fatigue. When I say fatigue, I mean, daily life. Fatigue is a woman and a man. Fatigue is a chair or a café. Fatigue is shadow and darkness. It is also the moon and sun.

These days, these days of fatigue, have their own books, each step a word. And the words do not end.

The other face / a mixture bonding, breaking apart, bonding in a circular motion that never ceases. And each face is lonely even when it embraces another.

The other face / the immediate presence rises to the level of poetry and dream. You want to embrace this reality, to inhabit it, because the fabric is the same, the space is the same, but each step has its own rhythm and its own horizon. The other face / the debate between estrangement and union, presence and absence. And so when you walk the Hamidiya souk it's as if you see things and you do not see them, as if you are seeking what you do not see in what you see.

RED

On a rug of red, of roses and anemones, the colors worship in the garden of our small house. Red is a fabric—some of it is a sheet for the place, some a shirt for time. When red wears its crown and climbs the ladder of the seasons, the earth waits for it on its green bed.

Oleander tree—each of your branches sways in waves, carrying red howdahs. Tenderly I listen to you, lips trembling among their leaves.

Red is the sun's throne.

CAFÉ SHATILA IN RODHA

In the café a pregnant woman talks to her body. Next to her is a bare date palm about to dry up in sadness because it could not shade the woman. The neem tree in the corner bends flirting with a man sitting under it. From the nearby waves horses bolt out of the water and each of the sitters imagines them as his dreams. And in every corner there is a hidden hand dressing a wound. A light wind filled with the sound of organs, mixing with the sounds of bells that rise from the throat of the lottery ticket seller, greeting the customers.

The sun has not stopped mixing its rays with the trees and people as it painted the sea.

The café rests its head on the pillow of the horizon.

RUINS

The moon breaks its mirrors on the ruins as Beirut makes crutches out of blood and ashes and hobbles with them.

It's true. The sky has chains around her feet, and the stars have daggers strapped to their waists.

The day rubs its eyes, disbelieving what it sees.

Weep, Beirut, wipe your tears with the horizon's kerchief. You wrote the sky again, but you were wrong, and now your wrongs write you.

Do you have another alphabet?

THE STARS AT HAND

A legend repeated here by the villagers says that night in the summer becomes an enchanted person. He appears in the village throughout the summer, walking alone with his head bowed. He spends his day counting stars and plucking out comets.

❁

In the summer when the sky cleared I used to read the stars by interpreting the lines in my palm. And I had a friend who opposed me, who read the lines in his palm according to the stars:
We did not ask which of us was more scientific. We asked, which of us was more poetic?

He used to say: Poetry is nature.
I used to say: Poetry is the unknown dressed up in nature.
The difference between us was unsolvable, but we remained friends.

❁

The river dried up.
The ink that wrote the willows dried up. Clover, daisies, and wild chicory were not its only poems. Be kind, if you pass by, to these notebooks scattered among the hands of the drought. Be kind to the bowed necks of the reeds, their broken heights. Be kind to the branches of the weeping willow whose tears have abandoned them.

River, where is the horizon that stretched in your embrace?

No source, no basin. Mud all cracked up, breaking up into dust. Peace to the lagoons that
were beauty marks on your long throat.

Peace to you, river-grave.
What testimony can I carve for you and what do I write on it?

A fish dried up like a rock, lost among dust and pebbles,
brigades of ants . . . and other insects whose names I do not know,
and the days fall in layers on them like a colorless glue.
      This is the path I walked, coming and going
      to the river.

Tomorrow, I'll wake the horizon that sleeps under its eyelids,
      and I'll disobey the rules and repeat:
      The feet that walked this earth and disappeared will be replaced
      by more beautiful and kinder footsteps.
      I hear their sounds echoing the traces of the sun.

A CHILDHOOD BEHIND THE DOOR

Since childhood I have felt that I am walking a road whose destination still confounds me. The summer sun, despite its clarity, was another vagueness. My road—starting from Qassabin, that weeping rose in whose shade I was born—was a quest marked by hesitance, wariness, and confusion. I remember that I stepped out with the music of words that resembled prayers soon after I washed the face of the morning with cold water.

I used to become happy—not in reality, but in my imagination—thinking that I heard voices saying that the trees here walked alongside a lover when they heard his steps. Or that they say, in another delusion, they danced in happiness looking at a lover from inside their home, seeing him go past their windows.

As for the road, it was hard and scabrous, hard to cross even if one had goats' hooves instead of feet.

❁

We did not have a garden. The field facing our house always complained of thirst. Except in winter, its lips were always dry, its throat choked with dust.

❁

When I think now of my childhood days, I am amazed. I grew up among villagers in a simple rural setting. I never heard any of them speak of death as if it worried them or that they were afraid of it. They all spoke of it as another spring. And some of them—those who have experienced death in its different shapes in life—saw it only as a harmless coincidence, or an ordinary event.

I say I am amazed, and I ask how did it find me this innervation, this awareness of death? Why was I as a child constantly afraid of death, as if it waited for me in every step, in every motion?

I do not know how it happened, how little by little I began to understand the wisdom that the villagers unknowingly possessed and that I too began to acquire. I thought perhaps existence to them was a single structure, or a single body like a poem: Life the beginning and death the end, in the same way that prelude and closure in a poem are a single wave.

Is my nature winter-like, and the other seasons merely images and improvisations?

I ask because I think of death as the winter of creation, and because the old anxieties return, especially in summer.

❀

This moment in summer, under this tree, and among the village children, reminds me of a moment in spring—the beginning of spring, when we used to rush out trying to capture the rainbow as soon as its feet landed on our field.

I saw it in the tobacco field in front of our house. The rainbow stood on two poles, one rising from the field and the other far away, or so I imagined. The sun wore a transparent veil that only covered half of its face, a gray veil adorned with black and white threads.

There was no hare or spider web to remind me of what Rimbaud said about the rainbow he saw in a place he never named.

The tobacco had been harvested.

There were only a few grasses and plants lying leisurely on the field's naked body.

The colors of the rainbow mixed with the colors surrounding them: green, red, gray, yellow, and terracotta. All mixed within the eyes of the children who gathered to witness it.

There was a soft mist falling from the clouds' inkwells, messages sent to the fields.

Then the rainbow disappeared.

I felt sad and began looking for it. I imagined the place of its first pole and in vain tried to find its trace.

The clouds took over the sky and the sun sank in a bed from which it did not rise until the next morning.

I spent the whole day waiting for the rainbow's return, but it did not. I imagined that the weather itself had become a lake of tears.

❀

Farmers like trees among whose shade the sun comes to rest—

Earlier they carried the morning and broadcast it on their fields, even though the day was a holy day.

A holy day is not an arrival, one of them said.

A holy day is another travel into the things we cannot stop imagining and that never happen.

A holy day is not an answer, says another farmer, and adds, it is actually a question that takes the shape of a throat.

A holy day is our other body exiled inside our body.

A holy day is a field.

Farmers, their steps are ointments spread on the wounds of the road.

❀

Something from my childhood still waits for me behind the door. I feel it whenever I come to my village Qassabin, but I never see it.

Once you told me, I'll wait for you behind the door—

You'll mix with my childhood. How will I distinguish you two then? I replied.

I expect nothing from time except that it becomes a shell closing on the pearl of meaning. Meaning supersedes time, flooding and hovering. Time is a vessel for storage, that's all.

Mix me in with you, dear image.

> Not a word from the sea has reached me this morning.
> Not a speck of night remains in my bed.

TO THE POEM

Will you not change the black dress you wear when you come to me? Why do you
insist that I place a piece of night in every word of you? How and where did you
acquire this droning power that penetrates space when you are only a few letters
on a piece of paper?

It's not old age, but childhood that fills your face with wrinkles.

Look at how the day rests its head on the shoulder of the sun, and how in your company I
fall asleep fatigued between the thighs of night.

The cart has arrived, the one that brings the letters of the unknown to you.

Tell the wind nothing will bar you from slipping under my clothes. But do ask the
wind, "What kind of work do you do, and who do you work for?"

Happiness and sadness are two drops of dew on your forehead, and life is an orchard
where the seasons stroll.

I have never seen a war between two lights like the one that erupted between you and the
navel of a woman I loved in childhood.

Do you remember how I followed that war? And how once I turned to time and said,
> "If you had two ears to listen with
> you too would have walked the universe, deluded and disheveled,
> > no beginning to your end."

Will you ever change the black dress you wear when you come to me?

Migrations and Transformations in the Regions of Night and Day (1965)

1. 'Abdulrahman al-Dakhil (733–788 A.D.), an heir apparent to the Ummayad caliphate, fled Damascus when a popular revolt erupted in 750. The rebellion brought down the Ummayad dynasty and led to the establishment of a new one, the 'Abbasid. Al-Dakhil, also known as Saqr Quraish (Falcon of Quraish), managed to evade 'Abbasid spies and agents who were tracking him. He reached Al-Andalus (Muslim Spain) five years later after a perilous journey. Though most of his family members were found and executed by the 'Abbasid, al-Dakhil, believing himself a rightful heir to the caliphate, succeeded in establishing an Ummayad emirate in Córdoba that controlled most of the Iberian peninsula, which he ruled until his death. Ummayad control of the region lasted for almost three centuries.

2. An area on the outskirts of Damascus.

3. A part of Damascus, and an alternate name for the city.

4. Al-Khidr (the Green One) is a mysterious figure in Islam who is known as a guide to prophets and saints. He is especially revered by Sufis.

5. Jeirun: an area near the eastern gate of Damascus where a Roman arch stands.

Stage and Mirrors

1. Al-Fatiha is the opening chapter of the Quran.

A Time Between Ashes and Roses

1. Imruulqais ibn Hujr ibn al-Harith al-Kindi was one of the greatest poets of the Arabic language, considered by many to be the father of the qassida, and author of one of the famed seven mu'alqat (suspended odes). He was born in the Jahili (pre-Islamic) era, sometime in the sixth century, in Kindah, which is now part of Yemen. After his father, Hujr, the prince of Kindah, was murdered, Imruulqais ended his bohemian existence and set out on a quest to avenge his father and assume the throne. He sought help from various allies, ending up in the court of Justinian I in Byzantium; Justinian reportedly poisoned him after discovering that he had had an affair with a princess in his court.

2. Abul al-'Ala Ahmad ibn Abdullah ibn Suleiman al-Tanukhi al-Ma'ari (973–1057) was born in al-Ma'ara, Syria and is one of the great Arabic poets. He was a philosopher who embraced rationalism and rejected religious dogma and Islam's monopolistic claim on divine truth. He was the author of a large body of poetry and prose, and his best-known work is Risalat al-Ghufran (Epistle of forgiveness), believed by many to be a predecessor of Dante's Di-

vine Comedy. Al-Ma'ari, who lost his sight at the age of four from smallpox, practiced asceticism and was a strict vegetarian.

3. Junaid ibn Muhammad Abu al-Qassem al-Khazzaz al-Baghdadi (830–910 A.D.) is a leading Sufi saint who advocated a self-possessed form of Sufism as opposed to forms of ecstatic mysticism advocated by Hallaj and others. His teachings brought great renown to the Sufi movement in Baghdad and he became known as Sayyid al-Tariqa (master of the sect).

4. Al-Hallaj (858–922), born in the Fars region of Iran, is one of the greatest Sufi poets. A student of Junaid, he was imprisoned and later executed in Baghdad for claiming self-divinity during the reign of the 'Abassid caliph al-Muqtadir. His best-known work is *Kitab al-Tawasin* (The book of talismans).

5. Muhammad ibn 'Abdujabbar ibn al-Hassan al-Niffari (d. 965). Although Al-Niffari is the author of *Kitab al-Mawaqif* (The book of standings), one of the most celebrated and most elliptical of Sufi texts, very little is known about his life except that he lived, taught, and died in Baghdad. It is also reported that his writings were not assembled by him, but by his son or grandson.

6. Abul-Tayyib Ahmad ibn Hussein al-Mutannabi (915–965 A.D.), was born in Samawah, Iraq, and is considered the greatest poet of the Arabic langauge. He was associated with several dynastic rulers in the region, such as Saif al-Dawla of Aleppo and Kafur of Cairo, for whom he wrote several odes of praise. These were followed by scathing panegyrics when relations were severed. Though often written in the form of praise odes, al-

Mutannabi's poems are chronicles of his age and demonstrate an unmatched command of complex Arabic syntax, a diction unrivaled in its richness, and a deep philosophical curiosity and insight.

7. Dajjal, meaning "false one," is the Arabic name for the antichrist.

Singular in a Plural Form

1. *Bahlul* is an Arabic term with several meanings, including fool, buffoon, and dunce, or, as the authoritative *Qamus al-Arab* states, "someone given to laughter." The word has other connotations, such as "simpleton" and "naïf," and is also associated with an individual who is so taken by the spiritual world as to be decidedly careless about worldly matters and appear stupid to others. The term's best translation is "wise fool."

The Book of Siege

1. Abu Nawwas al-Hassan ibn Hani al-Hakami (756–814) is one of the greatest poets of the Arabic language, known for his simple language and rich imagery and wit. Born in Ahwaz to Persian-speaking parents living on the border of Iraq and Iran, Abu Nawwas served in the court of 'Abbasid caliph Haroon al-Rasheed, where he wrote numerous poems that celebrate male homosexuality and wine. Abu Nawwas became a figure of hedonism and mirth in the Arab folk tradition, represented by his several appearances in *The Thousand and One Nights*.

2. Abu Tammam is Habib ibn Aus ibn al-Harith al-Taii (796–843 A.D.), a great poet of the 'Abbasid. He was born in the village of Jassim in the region of

Horan in Syria. He traveled widely through Syria and Iraq and worked in several occupations before being appointed postmaster of Mosul. His poetry was known for its density and cerebral orientation. Once asked, "Why do you write what cannot be understood?" he replied, "Why do you not understand what is written?"

Desire Moving Through Maps of Matter

1. A transliteration of ض, a letter in the Arabic alphabet considered to be a consonant sound that only Arabic speakers can make and that distinguishes Arabic from other languages. Hence Arabic is called the language of Dhawd.

2. Abu Hamid Muhammad ibn Muhammad al-Ghazzali (1058–1111) born in Tus in the Khorasan region of Iran (he is also known as Algazel). He is one of the most influential theologians and philosophers of the Islamic tradition, esteemed by both the Sufi and Sunni orthodox traditions. His best-known works are *Maqasid al-Falasifa* (The aims of philosophers), *Tahfutt al-Falasifa* (The incoherence of philosophers), and *Ihya 'Ulum al-Deen* (The rejuvenation of the sciences of religion).

3. Jean de la Fontaine (1621–1695) is a renowned French fabulist and poet. His best-known work is *Fables Choisies*, which he expanded and published several times.

4. Michel Simon (1895–1975) was a renowned Swiss-born French theater and film actor. Simon had a great affection for animals. His home on the outskirts of Paris was famous for its menagerie, including dogs, birds, cats, and five monkeys. Alexandre Bisson (1848–1912), French playwright and

novelist, known mostly for his 1881 three-act vaudeville *Un Voyage d'agrément.*

5. Louis Antoine Léon de Saint-Just (1767–1794), a French military leader and revolutionary. He served in Robespierre's Committee of Public Safety and was executed with him for his involvement in the Reign of Terror. Georges Danton (1759–1794), a leading figure in the first stages of the French Revolution. Seen as a moderate among the Jacobins during the Reign of Terror, he served on the Committee of Public Safety and was executed by the advocates of revolutionary terror.

6. Gérard de Nerval (1808–1855), a Romantic French poet, essayist, and translator.

7. Here the poet is referring both to the Littré French dictionary and to Émile Maximilian Paul Littré (1801–1881), the French lexicographer who assembled *Dictionnaire de la langue française.*

8. Barada, a river that used to run through Damascus. It has dried up in recent years.

9. Sanaa is the capital of contemporary Yemen.

10. Sheba here refers to the ancient name for Yemen, and of a region in contemporary Yemen.

11. Abu Firas al-Hamdani (932–968) was a poet best known for poems he wrote during his captivity by the Byzantines, who imprisoned him in 959 and 962. He was a member of a dynasty that ruled an emirate that dominated northern Syria and Iraq during the 'Abbasid era, and he was governor of the region of Manbaj on the Euphrates River. He died in battle fighting his cousin for the reign of their emirate.

12. The palace of Ghamdan once stood in Sanaa and was considered an architectural marvel. It was

destroyed by the caliph Othman ibn 'Afan, whose rule extended from 643 to 655 A.D.

13. *Ikleel al-Hamdani* (Hamdani's laurel crown), a book on Yemeni history and the genealogy of its tribes that outlines early Arab and Islamic history. Though its publication date is unknown, it is believed to have existed for several centuries.

14. Belquis is the Arabic name for the biblical queen of Sheba.

Celebrating Vague-Clear Things

1. See pages 396–97.

2. Barada is a river in Damascus, now dried up.

3. Pronounced "wawu."

4. See note about al-Ma'ari, page 395.

Another Alphabet

1. In the Damascus dialect, Al-shaddad is the name for a hair removal gel made with melted sugar, water, and lemon juice.

2. Al-Ghota, also known as Ghotat Dimashq, is an area of orchards and farms on the east and south of Damascus long celebrated for its beauty and fertility.

3. Wadah of Yemen is the poet 'Abdulrahman ibn Ismail al-Kholani (d. 708 A.D.), who hailed from Yemen. He joined the court of the Ummayad caliph al-Walid ibn 'Abdulmalik. Wadah, who was known as one of the most handsome men of his time, had developed an amorous relationship with the caliph's wife, Um al-Baneen. When informed that Wadah was in Um al-Baneen's chambers and that she had hidden him in a storage box or a trousseau, the caliph ordered that the box be buried.

4. Jareer Abu Harza Jareer ibn 'Attiya al-Yarbou'i al-Tamimi (d. 729 A.D.) was one of the best-known poets of early Islam, famed both for his odes of praise and his scathing panegyrics. Al-Akhtal is the poet Ghayath ibn Ghouth ibn al-Salt ibn Tariqa al-Taghlabi al-Wa'ili (b. 640 A.D.). He was also a poet of the Ummayad age and served as the principal court poet during the reign of 'Abdulmalik ibn Marwan. He composed numerous poems attacking the Ummayads' enemies and all who challenged their right to the caliphate. A contemporary of Jareer and al-Farazdaq, Al-Akhtal, who was a Christian, was engaged in several exchanges of panegyrics with the two. Al-Farazdaq is Hammam ibn Ghalib ibn Sa'sa' al-Darimi (658–728). He is one of the best poets of his age, widely known for his panegyric exchanges with Jareer that lasted for over half a century. He wrote praises of the Ummayad caliphs but leaned toward granting the caliphate to the offspring of the prophet Muhammad.

Dhil Rimma is Ghailan ibn 'Uqba ibn Nahees ibn Mas'ud al-'Adawi al-Rababi al-Tamimi (696–735), a poet of the Ummayad age, less renowned than the three above.

5. Ibn Taymiya is Ahmad ibn 'Abdulhalim ibn 'Abdulsalam ibn 'Abdullah Taqialdin Abul'abbas (1263–1328), one of the major scholars of Islam and whose influence is still felt. Living in Damascus during the Mongol invasion, he became a member of the school founded by the great Imam Ibn Hanbal (one of the four principal imams of Sunni Islam) and sought the return of Islam to its sources in the Quran and in the traditions of the prophet Muhammad. Ibn Taymiya's teachings remain a ma-

jor inspiration for the Wahhabi movement and ideology and its followers in Saudi Arabia and elsewhere.

6. Qassiyun, a mountain overlooking Damascus.

7. [*Excellence in the Science of Farming*] by Abdulghani ibn Isma'il al-Nabulsi (1640–1731).

Prophesy, O Blind One

1. Jim Morrison (1943–1971) was the lead singer and lyricist for the rock band the Doors.

2. This image of the heifers alludes to the biblical and Quranic stories of Joseph. Joseph is released from jail after correctly interpreting one of the Pharaoh's dreams, in which he sees seven emaciated heifers devour seven fat, healthy ones.

3. Jacques Berque (1910–1995) was a French Islamic scholar and sociologist.

Regarded as the most important poet writing in Arabic today, Ali Ahmad Said Esber, known to readers as Adonis, was born in a rural village in Syria in 1930. He was unable to afford formal schooling for most of his childhood, so his early education consisted of learning the Quran in the local *kuttab* (mosque-affiliated school) and memorizing classical Arabic poetry. He graduated with a degree in philosophy from Damascus University and went on to earn a doctoral degree in Arabic literature from St. Joseph University in Beirut.

Adonis's publications include twenty volumes of poetry and thirteen volumes of criticism. His dozen books of translation to Arabic include the poetry of Saint-John Perse and Yves Bonnefoy, and the first complete Arabic translation of Ovid's *Metamorphoses* (2002). His multi-volume anthology of Arabic poetry, *Diwan al-sh'ir al-'arabi*, covering almost two millennia of verse, has been in print since its publication in 1964. Adonis's many awards include the International Poetry Forum Award (Pittsburgh, 1971), National Poetry Prize (Lebanon, 1974), Grand Prix des Biennales Internationales de la Poésie (Belgium, 1986), Prix de Poésie Jean Malrieu Étranger (France, 1991), Prix de la Méditerranée (France, 1994), Nazim Hikmet Prize (Turkey, 1994), Lerici-Pea Prize (Italy, 2000), Oweiss Cultural Prize (UAE, 2004), and the Bjørnson Prize (Norway, 2007). In 1997 the French government named him Commandeur de l'Ordre des Arts et des Lettres.